Some Girls

First published by GALILEO PRESS in 2025

ISBN 978-0-913123-48-5

Several of these essays previously appeared in *Entropy*, *Cagibi Lit*, and *New York Tyrant*.

Book design by ADAM ROBINSON

Cover design and artwork by DECADENT WEST

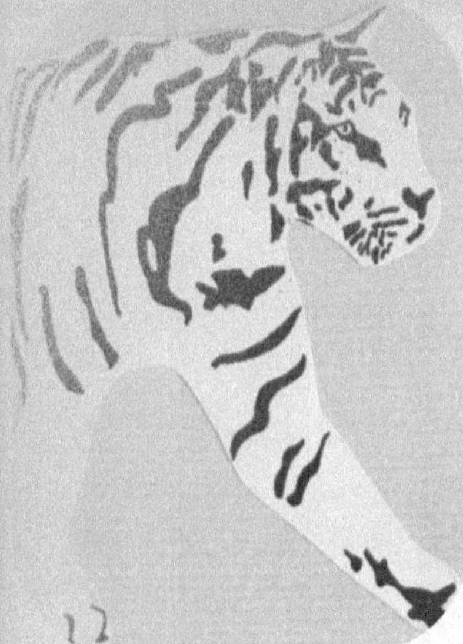

Some Girls

essays

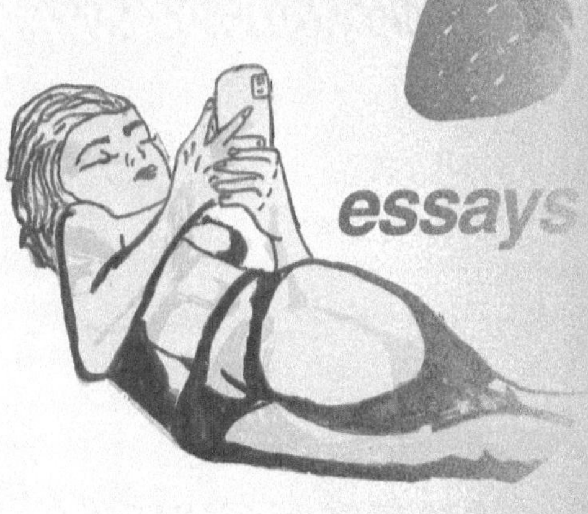

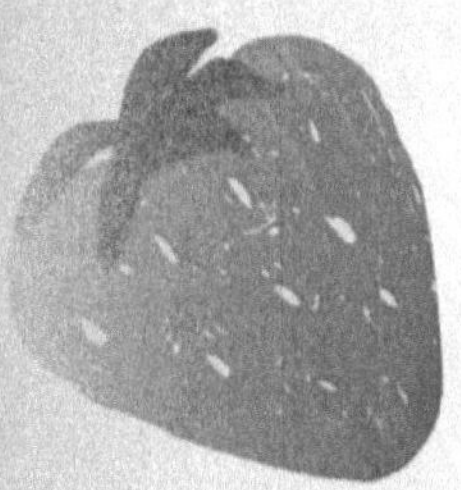

Emily May

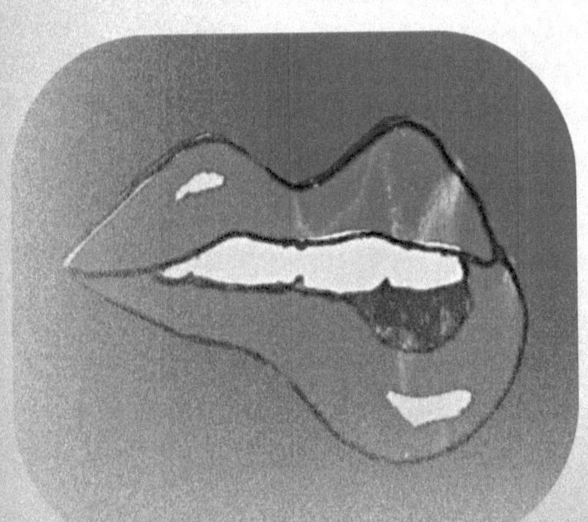

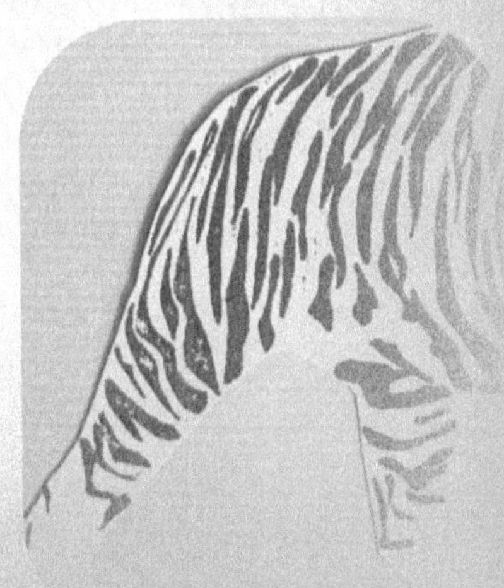

GALILEO PRESS
South Carolina

For Mom and Els

"American girls want everything in the world
you can possibly imagine"

—MICK JAGGER, *SOME GIRLS*

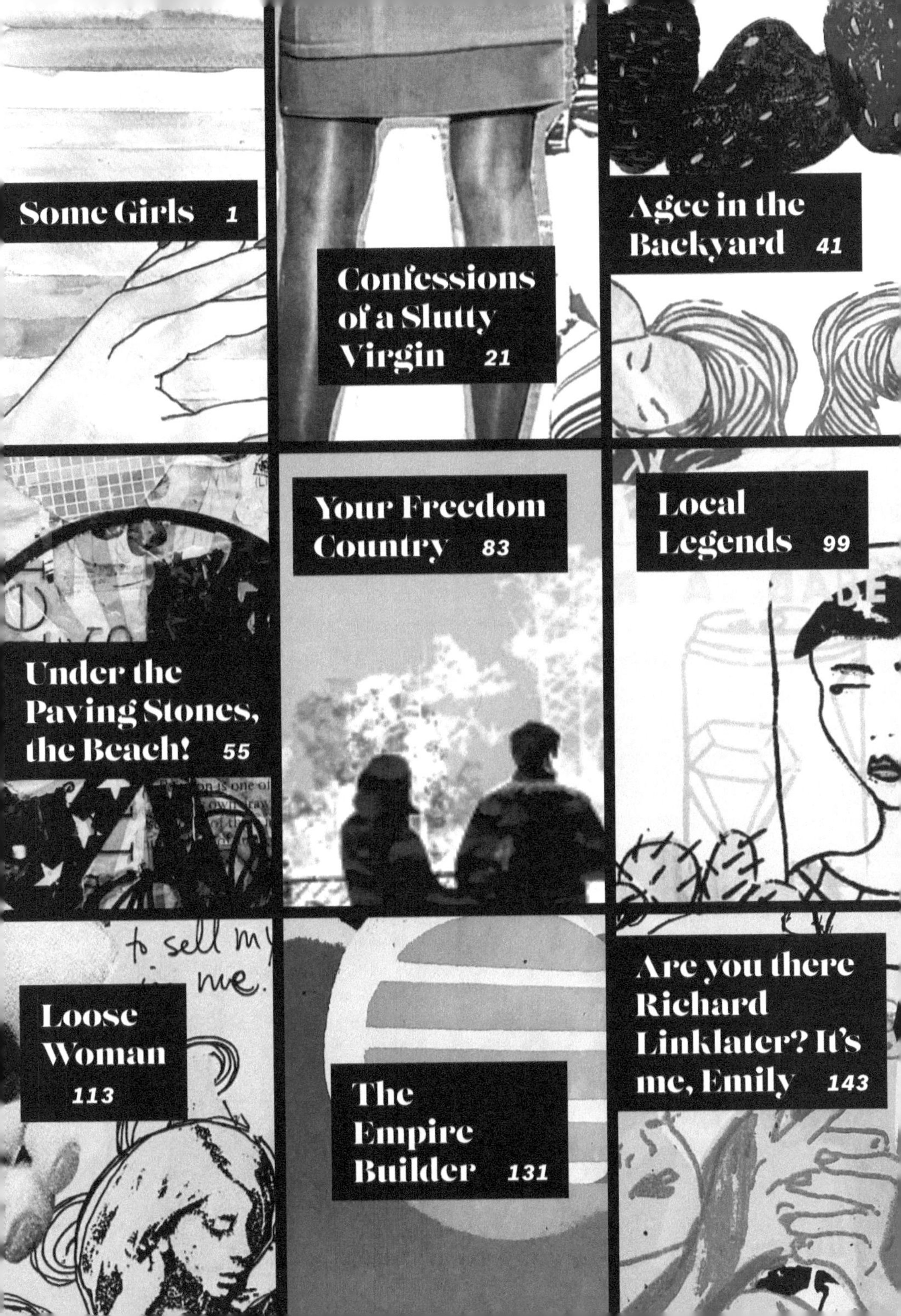

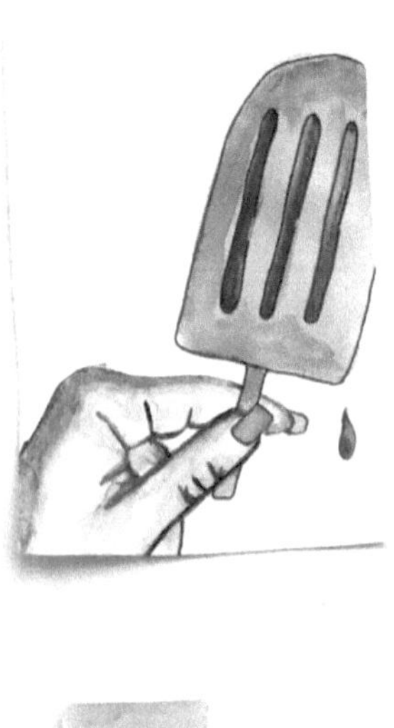

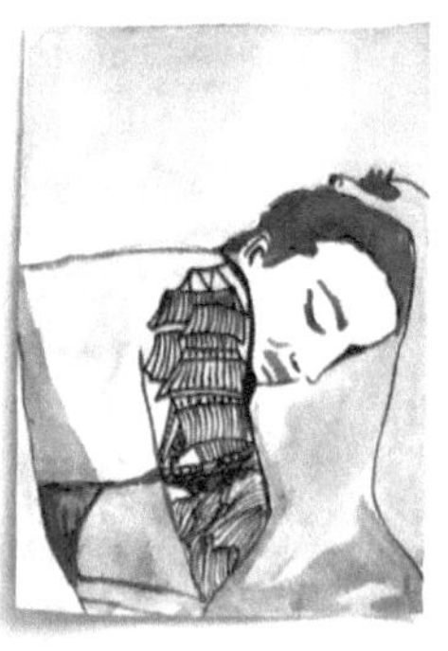

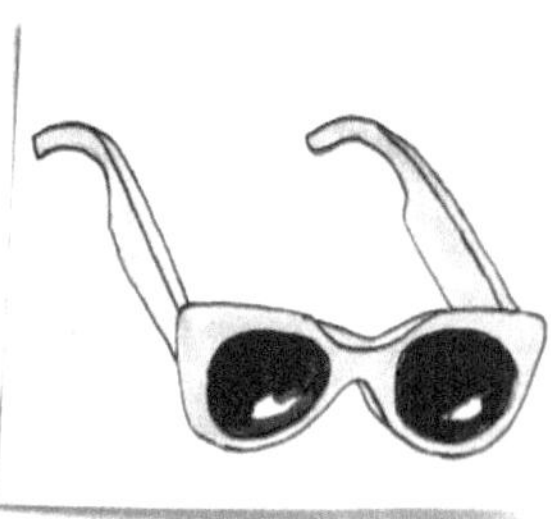

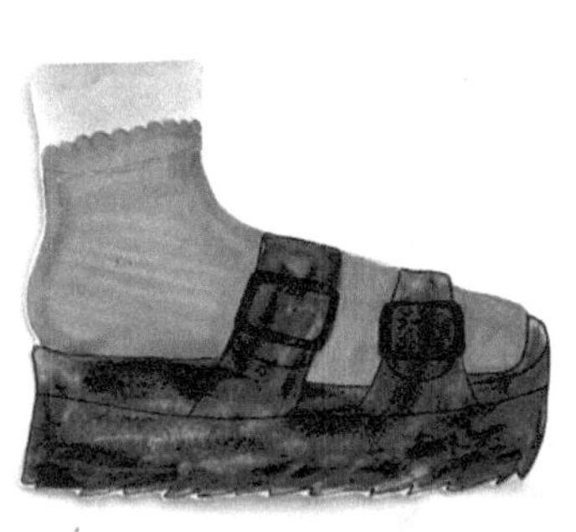

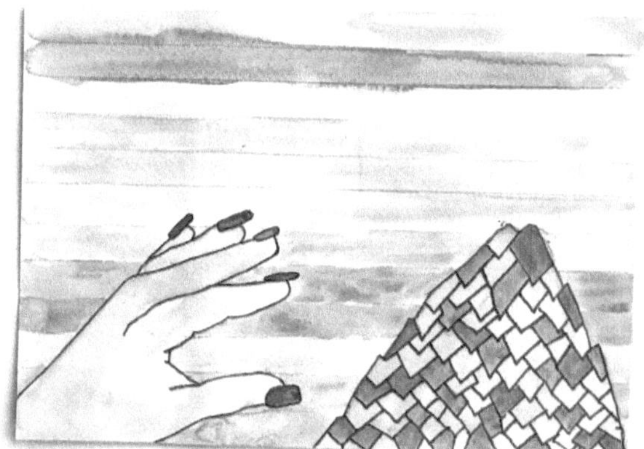

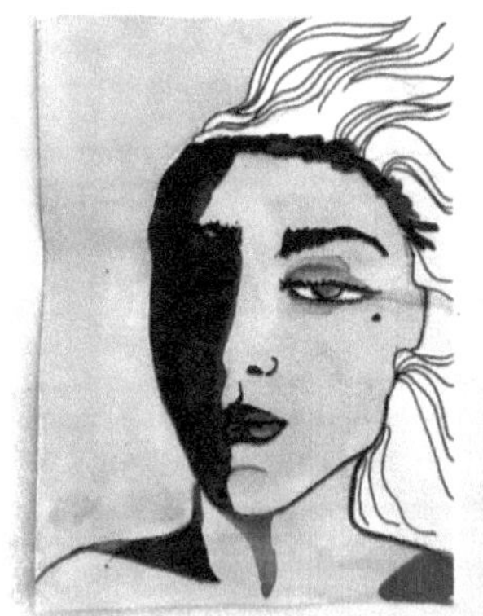

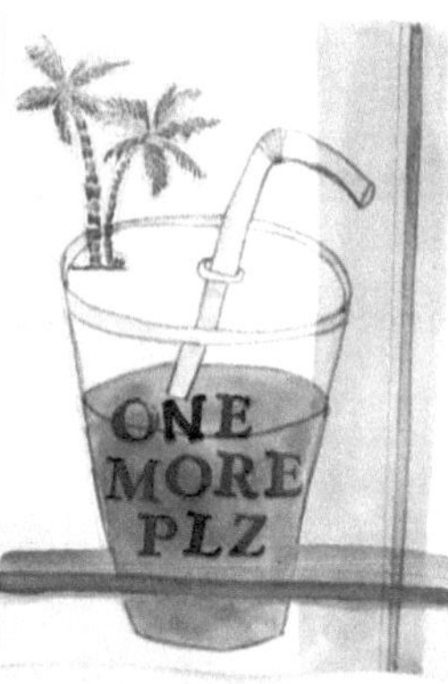
ONE
MORE
PLZ

Some Girls

Artists often speak about books and paintings and plays and songs as being *inside* them—as if they could be cracked in the right place and the art would crawl out, slowly at first and then quickly, fully formed. An Athena assuming the shape of self-realization. I've always liked this idea: that any one of us could be cracked in the right place and something revelatory could be pulled out.

At five or six, I asked my mother when the world turned color. We had black and white family photos in frames around the house, and I'd seen old movies and TV shows. When did the world that I was born into, the finished world, begin?

It was the nineties. Everything would keep getting better.

If my mother was a writer, she would have scribbled down her wonder at my question, and the process of watching something she created grow into something else entirely: something that would craft this observation of the order of the world, whose understanding of reality extended only as far as her own arms. But my mother wasn't a writer. She had three kids to take care of, and laundry and dishes to clean, and stacks of library books to pile into a red wagon for the walk home, and after all of that, even more work to do.

She laughed, and told me that it was always in color.

I tried to imagine that old world like the one I could see.

Athena, as the myth goes, was born fully formed from the head of Zeus. Zeus swallowed Athena's mother, Metis, and then developed a splitting headache: out cracked Athena, in full armor, as the goddess of war, handicraft and reason.

Was my mother Athena, or was I hers?

It struck me for the first time as a teenager that I would keep aging forward, and that I could never go backward, reversing in time to belong only to my mother. Small enough to fit into a single sunny afternoon: the park after school, a snack she knew I liked, her large soft hand gently brushing my hair from my face, and a nap in the warm room I shared with my tiny dark-haired sister whom I always squeezed tightly.

I would never go back to that place of short school days and freshly cut bangs, and I began dreading growing older. Becoming fully formed didn't guarantee armor, or prowess in war or reason. Adulthood meant accepting a life that existed in a house on a street in a town that when seen from above was a beige rectangle, indistinguishable from all the other houses on all the other streets. I wanted my life to be infinite, expanding far beyond the boundaries of salaries and yard maintenance. I knew that my mother loved me, that I was wanted, and this meant that I would be held tightly by the world in some way. I wanted to remain the child who wondered to my mother when the world turned color, believing that I had been born into the best, finished version of the world.

"When I was 12 it occurred to me for the first time I might have an interesting life," wrote Chris Kraus in *I Love Dick*. When I was twelve, I wrote in my journal: "I'm doing crunches and things so I'm fit for bathing suit season. Maybe I'll get a bikini!"

I also wrote: "Am I a completely different person than I was now that I am in fifth grade? Did I think other thoughts and breathe other air? Did I have a different mind? I read the entries from 'long' ago, and it's so different. Maybe in 2 more years I'll be a different person from now. But I don't want to be! Why can't I stay the same?" To change the body, and keep the self. The young girl's Cartesian dilemma.

During a recent summer, each day brought with it the increasing clarity that the dismemberment of the world we knew was nearly complete. The days topped a hundred degrees, and I walked the sidewalks in a daze. The sense of decay was so acute that I wondered how my own hair kept growing. Black roots emerged from my skull, thick black curls from beneath my black boy-cut briefs. On my walks through the dense afternoon heat, electric greens and their attendant orange blooms insisted we were both still alive, and I wondered how, or why.

I missed most the feeling of unfurling, of sighing and letting the world back inside me, of falling in love each night with the sun's painting of the clouds.

I took walks around the neighborhood listening to Brian Eno: *I scramble in the dust of a failing nation.*

This process of cultural dismantling was a surgery performed with blunt instruments, chopping away traces of *hope* or *the future.* And yet my body remained. My head hurt like I had eaten Metis too. Maybe I could give birth to something brilliant. I tried to coax something from my own mind, something other than the endless feed of our own destruction.

During this season of annihilation, I felt like getting fucked. It was one reason to be alive, and better than most. Lying under the man I share a bed with, I became a desperate animal, mewling softly for him as he wriggled out of his shorts and into me. We chopped scallions together in the evening, and he pulled me close each night when we got into bed, even when it was too hot and our legs were gummy, sticking to each other. I let my eyes roll back into my head as he hovered stiff-armed above me, like I was a surfboard and he was paddling toward some horizon. Or maybe I was the ocean, lapping up onto the shores of him. He would screw up his mouth to one side as he moved inside me, carefully and slowly, like he was carving something out. He folded his hands to say a silent prayer at dinner when he thought I wasn't looking, because I know god is fake but he's not sure.

"Religion has taken millions of lives, and there's not one person in heaven," I say. "That's the highest thought of all time," he responds.

We listened to "All Things Must Pass" on the turntable, and read each other's horoscopes. *Virgo: build a dream home for all your*

fears and set it ablaze. Taurus: whisper "I love you" into the ear of
your greatest enemy and mean it.

I gave up yoga for fucking on the weekends. He bent my leg further back behind my head as he explored further, seeing what else he could find deep inside me. I liked the feeling of being completely overpowered by what existed between us—rocking back and forth while looking into his eyes as they intently gazed back down at me.

This is having a body.

Afterward, I'd crawl on top of him, he'd wrap his hand around the back of my neck, roughly rubbing my hair, the motion turning arhythmic as his body settled toward sleep.

On a bright gray day when the summer greens grew darker, I imagined while lying there that the clouds would break as the sun dropped closer to the roofs of the buildings: a warm, sherbet-hued curtain dropping on the weekend. Something so pastel and innocent that I remembered the feeling of being a safe and satisfied child rather than an adult woman with a man breathing peacefully on her damp chest. But maybe it was wrong to consider those two states opposites at all. I rubbed his freckled shoulder before resting my chin on the top of his head. The rain never came.

New lipstick. Going to the bar instead of thinking about mortality. Growing full on the love you harvest daily. You are just a human who needs to feel happy sometimes.

A woman from the state I live in was sent to prison for self-inducing an abortion.

The state I live in declared a ten-thousand-dollar bounty on anyone who has an abortion.

I'm supposed to get my period today, but it hasn't come yet. It's never late. I look at the clock, try to feel the faint onset of cramps. Nothing.

I'm going to New York in a few days to see my sister. Should I get an abortion while I'm there, on her birthday?

This, too, is having a body.

We are advertised cellulite creams when we should be seizing the state.

One summer night a few years ago, I wrote in my journal, "The last abortion in Texas will occur at 11:59, one hour and seven minutes from now. I can imagine the anxiety of the women waiting: to see if they'll be admitted in time, worrying if they'll be attacked on the way out, sued later or imprisoned because of someone else's decision."

An idea for a thriller: a woman who goes out of state for an abortion tells a friend. The woman doesn't feel guilty about it, she's just like *yeah, it's fucked up I had to get on a plane.* The friend, short on cash, decides to turn in the woman for the $10,000 bounty that the state provides. Then it's a cat and mouse, maybe with a car chase. Like *The French Connection* but with women who speak. It's about betrayal and also making a salient political point. Hollywood will love it, get a rapist to produce. Or whatever, maybe an "as the father of daughters" guy. Maybe one of the White Chrisses could play the prosecutor, and maybe the twist is that he's in on the bounty too. Or maybe! He's the father. *And* the prosecutor! His performance will be tortured, Oscar worthy.

The woman in my state was let out of prison on half a million-dollar bail and the district attorney dropped the case.

In *I Love Dick*, Chris Kraus says, "what happens between women now is the most interesting thing in the world because it's the least described." I also wonder: What about what happens *to* women? I think about how each of us is being killed a little more each day: by bad news, by imprisonment for having a body, by dreams that are meaningless now.

I listened to news coverage of a garden-variety right-wing politician calling for a federal abortion ban. When the hosts of the segment presented the ideal alternative as leaving it up to the.... *state*, I realized I was dumbly expecting them to say "the person in question." I reeled for a second at the dizzying disconnect between freedom and reality, the yawning gulf that swallows up lives, and bit the inside of my cheek until I tasted blood.

Is there a phrase more condescending than *strong woman*?

I felt old at age eleven. It was my first season of reading magazines. I read an issue of *Seventeen* that had a fourteen-year-old model on the cover. If *she* was on a magazine cover, representing her prime, what hope did a fifteen-year-old have, as the sun was already setting on her? It was clear my time was already running out.

Young girls are set up to cannibalize each other this way: As the young models were consumed by all the corporations and the leering photographers they were beholden to, the rest of us normals were being devoured by the expectations that these girls had unwittingly set for us. *You can never be too rich or too thin,* they say. I would add that you can never be too young. The ideal woman is an underweight six-month-old heiress.

The semiotics of femininity is that of petiteness, suggesting the ultimate end goal is willing ourselves out of existing at all. The less there is to a woman, the better she is at being a woman. Whoever gets the closest to completely disappearing wins the prize. Being small, and becoming smaller, is all that's ever sold to us.

As a teenager, It seemed to me that being desirable to boys was an annoying, arduous process of playing a trick—present them with a fantastic image and then work constantly to maintain it: arrange yourself into something they'd like. Present a body but make the person disappear.

Every new generation of women has to learn again how to become selves, the progress always disrupted by the allure of becoming something that seems like it will be easier: a pretty ornament.

The Man I Live With doesn't understand that when I say I look like the portrait of Dorian Gray or that I need a boob lift as I pull my bra straps up in front of the mirror, I am engaging in the time-honored, culturally venerated sport of feminine self-deprecation. "I'll lift them for you," he says. He seems unencumbered by any sort of timeline whereas I fear it is too late for me to produce anything of value, as my psyche and ass in their marketable states are rapidly diminishing. This is the unassailable difference between us, a gulf. His impending fortieth is a cause for celebration; mine, a few years away, looms like the end of something.

I participate willingly in this cruel game against myself. I like the slight crinkles around his eyes; I think they are sweet, endearing, a sign of well-earned masculine wisdom. I like my own face only when the mirror can confirm that my lines are fine, barely there. Looking at one's neck in the wrong light and seeing lines there could convince one to feel like a ball that has been thrown up into the air and is on its way plummeting back to earth: that they are on the dying side of life now, useless as a natural artifact. But of course one would never descend into such thinking.

And yet the endless echo remains: *I'm doing crunches and things so I'm fit for bathing suit season. Maybe I'll get a bikini. Do I have a different mind? I don't want to change.*

"A woman must continually watch herself," says John Berger in *Ways of Seeing.*

> "She is almost continually accompanied by her own image of herself. She has to survey everything she is and everything she does because how she appears to others, and ultimately how she appears to men, is of crucial importance to what is

usually thought of as the success of her life. Her own sense of being in herself is supplanted by a sense of being appreciated as herself by another."

At the beginning of a new year, I pick up *Preliminary Materials for a Theory of The Young Girl*, written by the French philosophy collective Tiqqun. Debordian in nature, the book confirms on the first page what I have known to be true since my adulthood began: A war is being waged "that can no longer merely be called economic, social, or humanitarian. It has become total." What does the war look like? Movies are made by the Department of Defense, and the president that ruled over my entire coming of age made up a false justification to kill 100,000 people. Women still intentionally starve themselves. The banks failed and the only people who paid for it were those with the least. The success of total war means that we experience our resulting maladies (anxieties, depressions) as individuals rather than recognize them for the culturally inflicted mass ailments they are, Tiqqun says. We have missed that the Empire has conquered us all through the "molecular diffusion of constraint into everyday life," and conveniently for Empire, we mistake this war for our personal problems. The book identifies "girlitude" and 'youthitude" as the two most valuable—and exploitable—qualities one can possess.

When the Man I Live With and I first got together, I was thirty-three. I ruefully, jokingly, mourned the fact that my boobs were already past their prime, not quite as perky as even a few years before. My own eye acting just as it is supposed to: as an agent of Empire, demeaning and diminishing my own humanity even to myself. I gamely rendered myself another casualty of total war, successfully turned myself into an object. And I wondered how the gains of modern feminism seem to have been whittled down small enough to fit into the goal of Empire: it has granted us the freedom to celebrate ourselves as objects. And to protest being one is to take the form of a sexless humorless scold—a crone who has sacrificed her value as an object for something as meaningless as her own humanity. What would Athena say?

Over the course of my adulthood, cosmetic surgery was destigmatized first, then rendered empowering: It is every woman's right to turn herself into a more aesthetically pleasing object. I watched as this occurred while anti-abortion activists across the country ramped up their efforts. It was a crafty sleight of hand, and I knew we'd lost something elemental: that we'd forfeited the right to believe we were selves at all, for the right to be consumed.

I search "under-eye correcter" and quickly close the tab. Spending my money on cosmetics to hide my human face is counter-revolutionary.

I began looking at *Vogue* and Harper's *Bazaar* when I was eleven. I was immediately entranced: it was 1997, and all the girls were skeletal and heroinly chic: thick bangs, heavy eyeliner, ribs poking through skin the color of chalk. Sometimes a nipple attached to a suggestion of a breast would be perched over a handbag in an ad. Another accessory. All those glossy volumes of models whose thighs didn't touch: the sharp gaze of the cameras burrowed deep into the minds of everyone who flipped through the pages.

Despite all that:

Of course I liked looking at my naked body in the mirror. Or I carefully posed until I thought it looked okay. Until writing this sentence, I did not pause to consider referring to my reflection in the mirror as "it." Actually, perhaps more than *liking* to look at myself, I considered it my duty as a woman to scrutinize my body in the mirror to make sure that everything was in the right place, to reason that I only looked wide because it was a fat mirror, and that pair of black jeans still fit. I turned those magazine cameras on myself, exactly as I was meant to do.

If I felt too bad about the mirror and my mood started to plunge into an echo of teenage panic, as a feminist I had to look until I made a flimsy sort of peace; the sloped curves of my thighs and stomach didn't descend into untamed convexity: it wasn't *that* bad. It was wrong to not be beautiful, but it was also wrong to care.

This is having a body.

As the government takes up arms to obliterate us, we say: *Actually, I've done most of it already myself.*

And wasn't that the ultimate goal of the state: to take the body, and make the person disappear?

Around the time I began to look at *Bazaar* and dread growing older, I studied Greek myths in school. I found a book of myths in the library with my mother, and we flipped through it together. One of the myths stood out from the others. Demeter, the goddess of agriculture, was very protective over her daughter Persephone. The gods used their power to trick the women, as usual, and lured Persephone away from her mother. The ground cracked beneath her, and she was quickly taken by Hades, the god of the underworld. As Demeter grieved her lost daughter, the earth grew cold and plants withered and died. Hades was ordered to return Persephone to Demeter to revive the harvest. But Hades struck a deal: while keeping Persephone captive, he had offered her six pomegranate seeds. He claimed that her acceptance of the seeds meant that she would be bound to him and the underworld for six months of the year.

The mother's grief; the blood red gems of the pomegranate seeds; the deceitful men who would stop at nothing to get what they wanted; the women merely their pawns: irresistibly rich lore to an eleven-year-old, barely mythical at all to me now.

I visited my sister in New York, and we saw a Hopper retrospective at the Whitney. His wife Josephine served as his life-long muse. As they both grew into old age, he continued to render her as a young woman, with a slim waist and perky tits. An Athena in reverse: a fully formed woman, who'd done all the work of growing, frozen in time at the will of her creator.

Hopper's painting skill and vast collection of work were impressive. But maybe he was just another cruel god.

My lips used to be fuller. I bite them out of habit: lodging my teeth in and pulling. I bite my lips almost to prove something:

maybe that nothing good can stay, that everything will be eroded soon.

What's the reward for longer fuller lashes, repaired and rejuvenated hair, younger-looking skin? To always be loved, to escape hardship, to never feel any pain?

I scroll through my phone; there's been another school shooting and if I subscribe now I can learn a cleavage secret.

Forgive me Karl Marx, I have sinned: I bought a bright red Chanel lipstick at the duty free in LAX and feel glamorous when I put it on.

I spend the weekends selling clothing that I screen-print with nude figures or "Defund God" across the chest. Couples stop by my table, the woman holding a shirt against herself, measuring her boyfriend's opinion, placing it back on the rack if he doesn't seem excited enough when she searches his face for approval. Whenever this happens, I try my hardest to look away, mortified for the woman as she silently asks permission.

In college I found paintings of nudes objectifying, ultimately flattening, any woman to her surface. I love the bold gaze of the nude in Manet's *Le Déjeuner sur l'herbe*, but contemporary viewers were skeptical of her assuredness and found her immoral. A bad faith viewer can never see the humanity in a nude woman, I considered, even if Lee Miller makes the photograph. But I eventually changed my mind and started making nudes of my own. I felt like the female figure had a right to be reclaimed and celebrated, more truly rendered by its owners. I took a figure-drawing class, turned my most successful line drawing of the model in repose into a screen-print, and adorned every surface I could find with her: upcycled fabric that I sewed into woman-shaped pillows, on prints and repeated as a pattern on clothing. I sold hundreds of versions of this nude woman. I turned drawings of my own mirror selfies into a screenprint, my own infinitely replicable ass printed on fabric and paper and ceramics. Portrait of the artist as an object: Is it art or is it decoration? When we turn ourselves into something that is consumable, is the subject rendered a mere object?

The hard-won practiced boldness of American women became bolder first due to our twentieth-century successes, and then seemed to double as a response to our loss of rights in recent years. When I sold clothing and art, the nudes were my most popular item: The women who stopped by my table wanted to wear the nude, to own the nude, to proclaim her like she was the flag of a nation we hadn't invented yet.

In *I Love Dick*, Kraus highlights the work of Hannah Wilke, the pioneering and under-heralded feminist artist. Wilke wrote, "To exist instead of being an existentialist, to make objects instead of being one. The way my smile just gleams, the way I sip my tea. To be a sugar giver instead of a salt cellar, to not sell out..." *To make objects instead of being one*: the point of everything.

Wilke's most well-known work is her self-portraits in which bits of chewing gum are affixed to her naked torso, tiny vulvas dotting her skin. Kraus notes that Wilke's partner, Claes Oldenburg, left her for another woman, changed the locks to their New York apartment and then sabotaged a retrospective of her work. At the Whitney, I saw some Claes Oldenburg work, a big sandwich made of vinyl. It's striking in its whimsy and easily identifiable as his. It prompted me to wonder why an artist like Wilke isn't afforded the same level of recognition, her deeply unique work as easily identifiable as Oldenburg's.

The men who insist that *women are in charge now:*

My college professor, who called himself a feminist and said that we should take getting leered and catcalled by men on the street as a compliment. He joked that he wouldn't "expect anything" from me when he bought me a drink.

The guy I briefly dated in my twenties who came inside me without asking, whom I grew to fundamentally dislike but stayed with in case I needed an abortion, because he was an engineer and I earned minimum wage at a bookstore and was in the process of applying for food stamps.

Every tech billionaire and state senator with an infinite well of bloodlust and power.

This is the world in color.

I watch women say "thank you" to their dogs and "sorry" to each other for occupying space in a public bathroom at the same time. It's clear to me that all of this exists on the same continuum as the bill that has been introduced in another state: that a man has the right to murder his pregnant girlfriend or wife if he has reason to believe she will terminate the pregnancy.

"There isn't much I take seriously and since I'm frivolous and female most people think I'm pretty dumb," wrote Chris Kraus. I can relate. I dream of writing pop songs about fucking on the clock and wanting no one I love to ever die. I wonder if realizing that anyone in the world would be lucky to slap your ass is beating the final level of girlhood. "I am nothing, and I should be everything": a Situationist slogan, a perfect pop hook, a girl's refrain in a better world.

It occasionally occurs to me that it's not our job to feel good about the world we live in—no one worth listening to ever has. It's our job to pick up a brick: to destroy, and to create.

On my walks around the neighborhood, I was powered by the dark chattering desire to reverse everything that was happening. I wanted all the women that were murdered by their boyfriends and husbands for leaving, or by the state by refusing them the medical care they needed, to be brought back to life. For everyone who'd been jailed for having a body to be rewarded with never having to work again, to be granted a life of peace on a turquoise and white island somewhere, free from laws that seek to destroy them—for everything that had been taken from them to be restored.

I wanted to explore the whole world, for no one I loved to ever feel lonely, to drink espresso at a tiled table in the Lisbon sun, for no kid to ever suffer, to stay up late sipping mezcal on a rooftop and still get nine hours of sleep. *To be a sugar giver and not a salt cellar, to not sell out.* To make sweeping statements about how modern life has stripped us of our humanity and to be proven wrong, again and again. More time and less work: freedom to move about the world. Complete liberation for myself and everyone I'd never met.

But maybe I wanted vengeance too.

I guess Mick was right.

Six unelected people with sovereignty over three hundred and thirty-five million lives decided that women are not people, and that our bodies in fact belong to the state. I go for a run at dusk. I attempt to build a little prayer from the setting sun, my breath, and songs that had once been a soundtrack to something like joy. *I salt and pepper my mango/ Shoot spit out the window.* The sun is still orange through the dark trees, glowing fiercely as it sinks deeper into the day. The world is in color, and the sun doesn't know that the country it casts its light on has abandoned the people who live in it.

A state is not a mother, or a lover.

Under this sun, I imagine women plummeting to earth, their lives crashing to the ground like planes from the sky. We only wanted everything in the whole world you could possibly imagine. To live in our bodies and to own the world. But our very own flesh and futures don't belong to us. We might all be left for dead, looking in the mirror at ourselves naked, hoping we're good enough for whomever we were taught to please, whoever will let us live, as we turn, searching for the best angle.

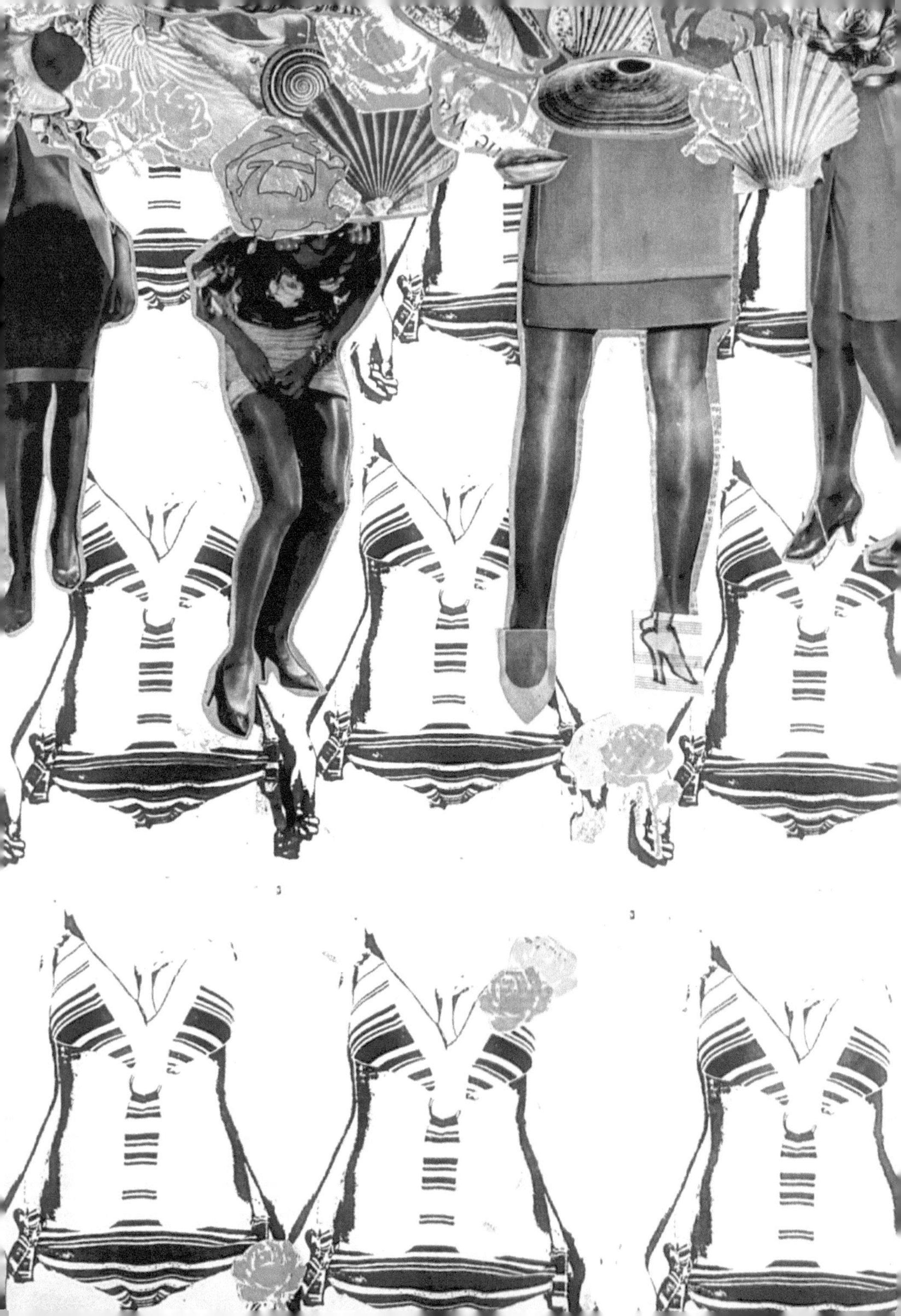

Confessions of a Slutty Virgin

The captain of my high-school cross-country team had bleached hair and a gap between his front teeth. I was in love with him in the way that only a fourteen-year-old-girl can be. One day, he told me that a new sophomore on the team liked me.

"Do you have any Irish in you?" he asked.

"No," I replied, confused.

"Do you want some?"

I couldn't conceive of the correct response to this question so I forced out a laugh.

I was a week into my first year of high school, not far from Philadelphia. I began preseason with the cross-country team as one of three girls in a group of twenty runners, and the only freshman. In the mornings, we ran on the wet freshly cut grass of the golf course in town, hopping up the hills and making up time on the straightaways. In the evenings, we circled the track as the day's heat settled, heavy and thick. When we weren't running, we played cards and watched movies. I tagged along with the older girls as they hung out with the boys, and tried not to embarrass myself while they talked about who'd slept with whom and which teachers were dicks. I felt like a child among adults. Their lives involved secrets and betrayal, and sneaking out of a boy's dorm room wearing his boxers. My life revolved around sleepovers with my friends and writing in my journal. I couldn't imagine ever being part of their world and wasn't sure I wanted to be.

The school had opened its doors to girls only one year before I arrived, breaking with one hundred and fifty years of tradition to maintain enrollment. In those first years, it wasn't so much a co-ed school but a boys' school that allowed us to enter. The buildings were old and solemn, built from stone that seemed ancient. The cavernous dining hall was lit with stained glass windows, its deep wooden walls dotted with N.C. Wyeth paintings depicting scenes from the civil war. The school colors were blue and grey, representing the brotherhood of the Union and Confederacy although the school was founded in 1851. This bit of trivia was meant to illustrate the significance of unity, the insidiousness of wearing the colors of the confederacy while we played sports never questioned or alluded to.

My dad was a science teacher and hockey coach at the school, his position allowing his children to attend free of charge. Aside from being naturally self-conscious from my years of mainlining teen magazines and extensive orthodontic hardware, I felt like I was under a microscope as Mr. May's daughter. I would have rather been invisible. As I began my first year, the girls were out-numbered by boys two to one. As girls we were all constantly scrutinized: who was hot, who was slutty, who wasn't that hot but still slutty, who *was* hot and *should* have been sluttier.

When preparing to bring girls into the campus fold, the school seemed to imagine that this would involve no structural changes aside from deciding which of the dorms to assign to the girls. The urinals that remained in all the bathrooms served as a constant reminder of who was there first and who ultimately owned the school, the world that contained our entire experience.

The walls of the athletic center, where we picked up our freshly laundered uniforms for cross-country meets, were lined with photos from the school's fifteen decades of history: legions of fit young white men, arranged in rows, with slicked-down side parts and varsity sweaters. The boys were frozen in the brief flash of their youth with their ancient haircuts and stoic glares. They looked solemn and sure, the absence of expression signifying masculinity and strength. The wide hallway smelled like ancient sweat and varnish, The young male faces stretched on for what seemed like miles.

If the school's administration felt there were any cultural changes that the school needed to implement, that the girls might need to be protected from an environment in which they were vulnerable outliers, they never let on. "Forging boys into men" had been the school's party line for decades, but they offered no analogue of turning girls into women. Perhaps they were unwilling—or unable—to wade into such uncharted waters. It seemed as if they realized they might have to revise the script entirely but didn't feel like putting in the effort and hoped we wouldn't notice. What made a woman was a question that the school seemed unwilling to ask, let alone answer. We were tacked onto the boys' realm: the boys wore dark blazers over the collared shirts, and we did too. The boys were expected to excel in both class and sports, and so were we.

The Classics building where I conjugated Latin verbs was unrenovated, each classroom lined with elaborate stacks of yellowing papers collected over the long careers of Latin teachers who'd been teaching for decades before I and my classmates were born. The dust that danced in the sunlight of the chilly early mornings seemed to have floated there for decades too, since only boys sat in these chairs, since Oliver Stone found his time in these buildings grim, Dickensian and "...scary. You did not deviate. And if so, you paid the price." Thirty-five years after his era, the girls were here: with short skirts, AOL Instant Messenger, and thirty minutes of unsupervised free time between study hall and check-in each night.

Late in cross-country season, the air turned cold and caught in my breath on our daily five-mile runs through town. I could feel the frozen air expanding in my lungs, piercing them, but the pain was worth enduring—for our team's shared pursuit, or maybe just to prove I could do it. The brilliant October yellow of the leaves had dropped to the ground, now an ankle-deep sea our team of a dozen runners rhythmically shuffled through together.

One of our last races of the season was a huge invitational in the center of the state: three point one miles through a bleached corn field, against hundreds of runners from dozens of other schools. The race was hours from our school, and only two other girls and I travelled with the boys' team. Lara and Clarissa were both seniors, and the three of us shared one hotel room while the boys had a full floor of the Red Roof Inn in Nowhere, Pennsylvania. The night before the race, we crept over to one of the boys' rooms to play cards while an inane movie played. The boys performed exaggerated playful violence for our benefit, slapping their cards and each other and yelling *fuck!* about everything. Lara and Clarissa laughed or rolled their eyes in response. They were both tall and beautiful, with long legs and long ponytails. I watched them closely, trying to learn how to be casual, without overthinking everything or being afraid that any wrong move would end up chiseled on my gravestone. "Here lies Emily, who didn't know that any white liquid was obviously presumed to be cum."

I was preoccupied with trying to seem relaxed in my tank top and sweats, sitting on a floral polyester bedspread in a hotel room with older boys, like this was every Friday night of my life. Chris, a Navy post-grad, decided we would order a pizza. After a few more rounds of cards, there was a knock on the door. Chris opened it, and the pizza guy stepped through the doorway. Chris took the pizza and handed over some rolled-up bills. The pizza guy was in his twenties, wearing baggy jeans and a scruffy beard. "Thanks, man," he said to Chris. "How much for her?" he nodded to me, still holding out the money.

"Man, get the fuck out of here!" Chris howled. He grabbed the pizza guy's arm, shoved him out of the room and slammed the door. "What the fuck was *that*?!" he shrieked, laughing, and punctuated it all with a cartoonish jump.

"He was scared of your muscles, Chris," said Lara. "Don't worry, Mily, we'll protect you."

"God, what a freak," said Clarissa.

I stood silent with my mouth open, unsure how I should react. Be cool or freak out? I was shocked, and briefly wrapped in a thick and tangled sense of flattery: this stranger, however crudely, had demonstrated my desirability in front of all these other boys. But then I felt ugly, because he was and he had chosen me.

A warmth toward Chris filled my body. I felt indebted and strangely drawn toward him: my protector. The depths of my animal brain knew he had slain my predator: I would live another day. But here in the human world of hotel rooms, the low glow of the TV, and ten-dollar bills wound tightly around each other, I wondered if I would always be for sale in some way, or at the whim of one man stepping in to protect me from the rest.

"Let's just play another round," I said.

Over winter break of my freshman year, my English teacher assigned us *Catcher in the Rye*. I was accustomed since elementary school to hate whatever I was forced to read for class, the assignment reliably stripping a book of the romance of choosing it myself. I read *Catcher in the Rye* in one sitting. Holden's anger and annoyance at everything around him reverberated, his voice snagging a part of me and echoing in my mind.

Catcher in the Rye, A Separate Peace, This Boy's Life: tales of alienated young men trapped in bleak institutions, painted in tones of brown and gray. The characters in those books were established as archetypes of teen angst, longing and rebellion. Holden's disgust at his world crackles on every page. Even at the time, I wondered: Where is the girl Holden? And could her anger span the entire reality she existed in, like Holden's, or would it only extend to the confines of being an accessory in a place like this, where the protagonists are always in their blazers and khakis, and the girls are left to flutter in the background in their regulation-length skirts, serving as plot devices? "Some girls you practically never find out what's the matter," says Holden. (*Some girls* again... I wonder now if this portion of Holden's monologue could be a lost lyric of Mick's own diatribe.) But did Holden ever *ask* those girls what was the matter? Most of all, where was an angry girl's voice that resonated, furious that life amounted to tricks to avoid snacking and seeking the approval of lacrosse players with nothing to say and no will to listen? Some boys you practically never find out what the point is.

As my first year became my second, I grew used to living vicariously through conversations I had with my friends about their meetings with boys in dark corners. I absorbed real-life experience from them, hoping for an osmosis.

These meetings seemed like a deeply unromantic, terrifying arrangement to me: they often involved no real-life flirting at all. Just a quick Instant Messenger conversation:

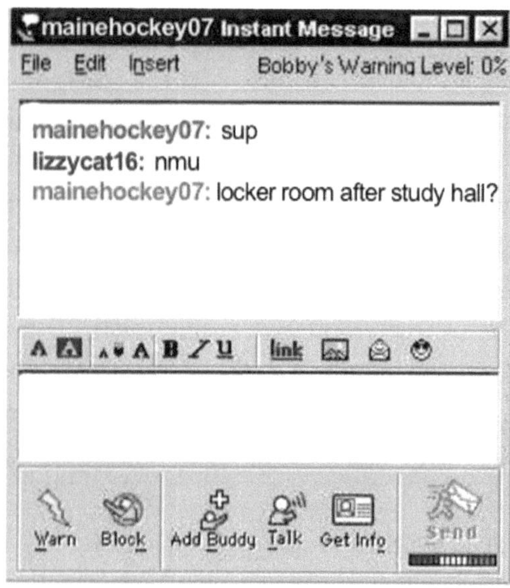

I couldn't name it then, but I was struck at the hollow and transactional way my friends would recap those quick liaisons afterward: just a rote description of swapping a blow job for getting fingered. He might ignore you in class the next day. The interaction served as the primary means of accruing the currency we all trafficked in: power.

My friends never mentioned that these liaisons were exciting or felt good, or that they even liked the boys. The implication was that they had secured their social standing as a desirable girl. Maybe to show up, to engage, was expected, and cool—but to *like* it was slutty. Playing the game was rewarded, but for girls to initiate or revel in these meetings was to risk becoming a social pariah.

Maybe the only way we could take part in our own story was to meet the boys after study hall. There, we could become a character, even if an antagonist, in the rumors that circulated on Instant Messenger when we all returned to our dorms, and in the halls the next morning.

The boys themselves constantly brutalized each other as we looked on. A popular insult they had for each other was *pussy-whipped*, as if there was anything else they could hope to be. A fabric hook on the back seam of an Oxford button-down was a "fruit loop": the absolute importance of adhering to an ever-changing code of heterosexual masculine dominance was ultimately so tenuous it could be diminished by the presence of a one-inch band of fabric.

But the boys weren't the only ones compelled to perform their gender. My own girlhood was purchased in the Juniors' department and at the Clinique counter, five pairs for $20 at Victoria's Secret. The thongs, we all insisted, were "more comfortable." We couldn't fully make ourselves disappear to fit the boys' preference, but our panty lines could. The lack of fabric there announced something tantalizing to those who gazed upon it, which perhaps comprises the bridge from girlhood to womanhood: that we were willing to sacrifice our comfort to convey *sexiness* while adamant that it was for *us*. If the goal for womanhood under patriarchal capitalism is ultimately the alienation of a woman from her *self* and her body, in order to be controlled equally by men and the desire of objects for sale, this is the moment she is first split: when she convinces herself the choices she makes under the duress of this system are *for her*.

But I wasn't thinking about any of that then. I woke up early each morning to apply eyeshadow and concealer and ironed my long hair bone straight. I dyed my hockey skate laces pink. I was insistent on something, and at the time I didn't know what. Girlhood was reified through the act of performance itself. To succeed at girldom was to perform all the labor required, and then convincing yourself *it's for me*.

In chapel twice a week, we all glazed over as the headmaster droned on about the storied tradition of our school motto, "Whatsoever Things Are True," whatever that meant. Our older male teachers and dorm parents, some of whom had been there since it was the monastery Oliver Stone had hated, were now faced with an unfathomably foreign new set of problems: teenage girls with the top few buttons of their collared shirts left unfastened. In a clunky effort to acknowledge that we as girls in fact faced different obstacles than the boys, the school switched up their mandatory programming. We had an all-school assembly in which a woman pointed out photoshopped photos of models. "Cindy Crawford said she *wished* she looked like Cindy Crawford," she told us. Another speaker talked to us about rape and how to avoid it, by peeing or barfing on our assailant. A boy in my class raised his hand to challenge her.

"Rape isn't real," he said. "A girl wouldn't be in that situation if she didn't want to be."

If the school was unprepared to address what made a woman, I'd have to educate myself independently. I searched the pages of teen magazines and the prevailing ideal of young women in the early 2000s: the songs and videos of Britney Spears, Christina Aguilera and a host of more disposable blondes. The basis of their collective *oeuvre* was a constant, sexy refrain of *yes but no, no but yes* while wearing pants with waistbands that rested half a foot below their belly buttons, indicting any of us who ate carbs. Christina trilled the words that a team of middle-aged Swedish men had written for her: *you better cross the line*. It was clear that desirable American girls should be slutty virgins, hot enough to tempt the boys but with no real desire of their own, handing the reins to the boys by default.

Meanwhile, the messaging around what slutty actually *meant* remained unclear. My friend Liz remarked that she thought girls who smoked weed were slutty, which confused me. What did weed have to do with sex? At the end of a hockey game one cold Saturday afternoon, after the final buzzer echoed through the outdoor rink, our team lined up to shake hands with the other team. One of our opponents decided to shove Ashley, our captain, before quickly skating away. Ashley blinked, stunned, then turned around and loudly shouted, "You're a slut!" at the other girl's back. I was confused again, as I couldn't square the idea that sluttiness could exist outside the realm of sex. I tried to make sense of the order of the world I inhabited into a sort of *whatsoever things are true* about sluttiness:

1. Girls could be slutty in a myriad of ways, with or without involving actual sex.
2. The insult (and it was always an insult) remained perpetually close at hand, to be wielded in any necessary situation, like a knife in a back pocket.

3. There was no earthly manner in which a boy could
    achieve sluttiness.

Gossip spread like a forest fire each morning in the student
center: which eighteen-year-old senior football player was fucking a fourteen-year-old freshman girl in the locker room, who
had hooked up in the Headmaster's Garden the night before.
("*Her* with him? She's such a slut!") I was often the one relaying everything I'd heard. Even though I constantly whined to my
journal about wanting one of these boys to like me (and then
immediately losing interest when they did), I would have chosen
to evaporate completely rather than have my name be whispered
in the hallways before first period, and I never came within a
hundred yards of letting a boy touch me. Or, even wanting one to.
But I still aspired to be a hot girl, with platforms and halter tops
at school dances. I applied bronzer and lip gloss, lined my eyes in
smudges of gray, gazed into the blinking eye of my Vivitar film
camera; teenage girls were taking selfies long before the iPhone. I
wanted to reproduce the full-lipped pout Britney, whose longing
would never go unsatisfied (or so we believed at the time): to
become real by replicating an image. The J.Lo lyrics on my AIM
away message (*my life I live it to the limit and I love it, now I can
breathe again, baby now I can breathe again*) suggested self-deter-
mination while calling out to some fantasy boy: another mirage.

I dreamt of being held close by a pretty man, being told I was
beautiful and therefore worthy of love and adoration. The feeling
of being *wanted* was the point, winning the game of attention
the erotic end. I wanted not the man or sex necessarily but more
so just to *be* wanted: to achieve power through the passive voice.

If I was wanted, my own desire could be allowed to emerge in a diluted or muted fashion. Maybe it was all of human history, maybe it was especially thick in 2001, uniquely pronounced at a boys' school that let some girls in, but every molecule we carefully moved through conveyed the truth that woman is object and man is subject, and that's how we became legible even to ourselves.

"Did you make the list?" my friend Drew asked me one morning in the student center.

My junior year, the boys ranked the top fifteen hottest girls in our class and were circulating a piece of looseleaf with a grid drawn in ballpoint pen. Attributes and drawbacks of the girls' looks, the amalgamation of who they were, were carefully detailed on the page. Face, tits, ass/no ass, legs, hair.

These were the cool boys, who maybe weren't on varsity teams but were funny stoners who left campus to smoke weed behind the pizza place on the weekends, creatively defied the dress code daily, were friends with the girls they ranked. To me, the list was proof that cruelty was embedded in the social DNA of teenage boys, and to expect anything more was to set oneself up for defeat. But they would surely say the same about us. For the girls who made the list, to protest even slightly against being reduced to a collection of physical attributes was not a reaction within the bounds of how we were supposed to act. The blondes who were on it rolled their eyes, maybe a little proud, a little hurt by the detractions in the notes (*minus .5 for being too tall, kind of a bitch, really dumb*).

I did not make the list. *These barbaric tools have no taste!* I thought to myself. But of course, there's no real pleasure in losing a game you've agreed to play.

The summer before my senior year, I traveled to South Bend to attend a literature program at Notre Dame. There were about a hundred and fifty seventeen-year-olds in the program, immersed in various subjects over the next three weeks. After unpacking in our dorm room, my roommate Brigid and I walked to the welcome assembly. Dozens of teenagers from across America quickly eyed each other up and down and decided who they would be friends with or try to make out with. There was a level of hormonal desperation that remained at a low hum for the first five minutes of orientation and then immediately accelerated to a boiling shriek. I would be goddamned if I didn't return to my friends at home with a story, finally.

Here in a new place, I wasn't a fac brat, or a prude. I was cute and tan and wearing size four plaid Abercrombie shorts that hugged my ass and had a two-inch inseam.

I immediately became friends with a group of about ten girls on my hall. We gossiped about everyone else and quickly named ourselves Team Bitch, and made T-shirts to announce our pack. Among my new friends were Amy and Savannah, vegetarians from California. I stopped eating meat because I thought they were cool. They were freer than my peers at school, less constricted by an environment that demanded uniformity. They were smart and sure of themselves, smoked weed casually and had devoted boyfriends who sent them letters while they were away for the summer. I tried to imagine the boys at my school doing something like that; somehow their heterosexuality still seemed to be male-centric, and sending a letter to a girl would somehow be too gay.

I met Josh after the first week. He was blonde and from Louisville. He wore a polo shirt, khaki shorts and white K-Swiss sneakers. A puka shell entwined in hemp rested in the center of his polo collar. In the moment, he was cute enough and seemed nice: He would do. On Saturday night, Josh and I went for a walk around a pond behind our dorms. A large statue of the Virgin Mary ushered us into this realm. The cicadas toiled frantically to produce a deafening song while we invaded their habitat. I drank in the Polo Sport Josh was drenched in, which excited every cell in my body. After we circled the pond, we shared a long, meaningful hug, the clear meaning of which was *I want to jam my tongue down your throat.*

The following Saturday night, we took another lap around the pond, talking about god knows what inanities: sports or siblings, where we wanted to go to college. After arriving back where we started, he pulled me close and our mouths found each other, and we plunged in deep. *Finally*, I thought. *I've joined the world. I have felt a boy's tongue searching around my mouth and begging for more. I know life.* I ran back to my dorm afterward to give Brigid a play-by-play, and she shrieked with delight before detailing her own romp with a vaguely European guy whom she'd been strolling campus with. A week later, on our last night on campus, Josh and I met up again. We were both fully aware of how weighty this moment was: it was the sexual equivalent of a fire sale. Everything must go. We ambled down the dark path to the pond in the soft stickiness of the midwestern summer night.

"Do you wanna skip the walk?" he asked.

"Sure," I said. We sat down on a stone bench under the statue of Mary. I sensed that anything could happen, and I was ready for it. I was wearing a fitted black tank top over my purple lace bra, and he was once again positively bathed in Polo Sport.

He admitted that the counselor in the boys' dorm bought them booze. "I'm kinda drunk," he said, lifting up my tank top and bra and brought his mouth to my nipple. I was exposed, too self-conscious to even consider that this might be enjoyable, but felt womanly. He proceeded to unzip his shorts, and I awkwardly fondled him without knowing what I was doing, relying on vague instructions from *Cosmo* that I'd been reading for years with the sole intention of being prepared for this very moment.

"What do you want me to do?" I asked (according to my journal, sexily).

"Do you wanna put your mouth on it?" he asked.

I opened up, and bobbed up and down, while he palmed the back of my head.

I worried briefly about the whole scene taking place *here* but ultimately decided *who cares*! I'd joined the world of teenage deviance, my bright and elastic veins coursing with life and something like desire. And I had a story to tell my friends at home, who were all lapping me in this contest of sexual conquest that had somehow been foisted upon us, and probably had been since human teenagers were walking upright. I left early the next morning but not before leaving Josh a box of Mike 'n' Ikes (which he mentioned he liked in one of our pond conversations) with a note saying I'd had a good time and have a good rest of the summer.

Back home, Josh and I became AIM buddies, which led to no memorable exchanges; his crude away messages turned me off but ultimately didn't surprise me. I had no illusions about a true connection; he was a story, which was equally as valuable. We chatted once or twice before I filed the experience away, mostly relieved that I had completed one level of girlhood and had finally ascended to the next one.

Team Bitch vowed to keep in touch, and we decided to write to each other in a shared notebook, which we mailed to each other back and forth across the country. A week or so after returning home, I received the notebook from Savannah, in Santa Clara. "We were all hanging out the last day after you left and Josh said you gave him head!" she wrote, which I read as an accusation. Was she... wondering if I had actually done it, and if I had, I was a slut?

It took me years after leaving high school to realize fully what a cage it had been, and that I had to unlearn most of what I knew. Now, more progressive voices in pop culture affirm the personal agency and pleasure-seeking impulses of teenage girls. (*Teen Vogue* of my youth: "Which Lipglosses To Buy So Your Crush Won't Notice How Fat You Are." *Teen Vogue* today: "Why Orgasming to Karl Marx Matters.")

Even today it seems ambitious to proclaim that the sexual proclivities of teenage girls are morally neutral. It's the knotty mess of an entire human history obsessed with girls' purity that renders a strappy tank top or whatever a teenage Britney Spears was doing as lurid. It seems that starving girls of their agency is the best way to create adult women who are half alive, who count calories and feast on shame, make themselves smaller in every way, but never small enough, trapped in an eternal state of deprived adolescence. (Britney herself couldn't even win the game.)

It feels almost impossible to read about a girl's sexual coming of age without holding your breath, waiting for the trauma. Maybe we even think she deserves it. Even I know I was lucky that it only involved a little bit of shame, that I got out easy. It's a tightrope walk for every girl, with swords beneath her if she falls and tigers waiting if she makes it across, while everyone watches, waiting for her to be impaled.

Because if teenage girls or women were allowed to have agency, to have desire and act on it—to be main characters—the fabric of civilization would deteriorate while roving gangs of girls set fire to the Constitution and God, and push buildings and the economy into the ocean.

"I can't believe Josh would make that up!" I wrote to Savannah in the journal before packing it up and sending it back across the country.

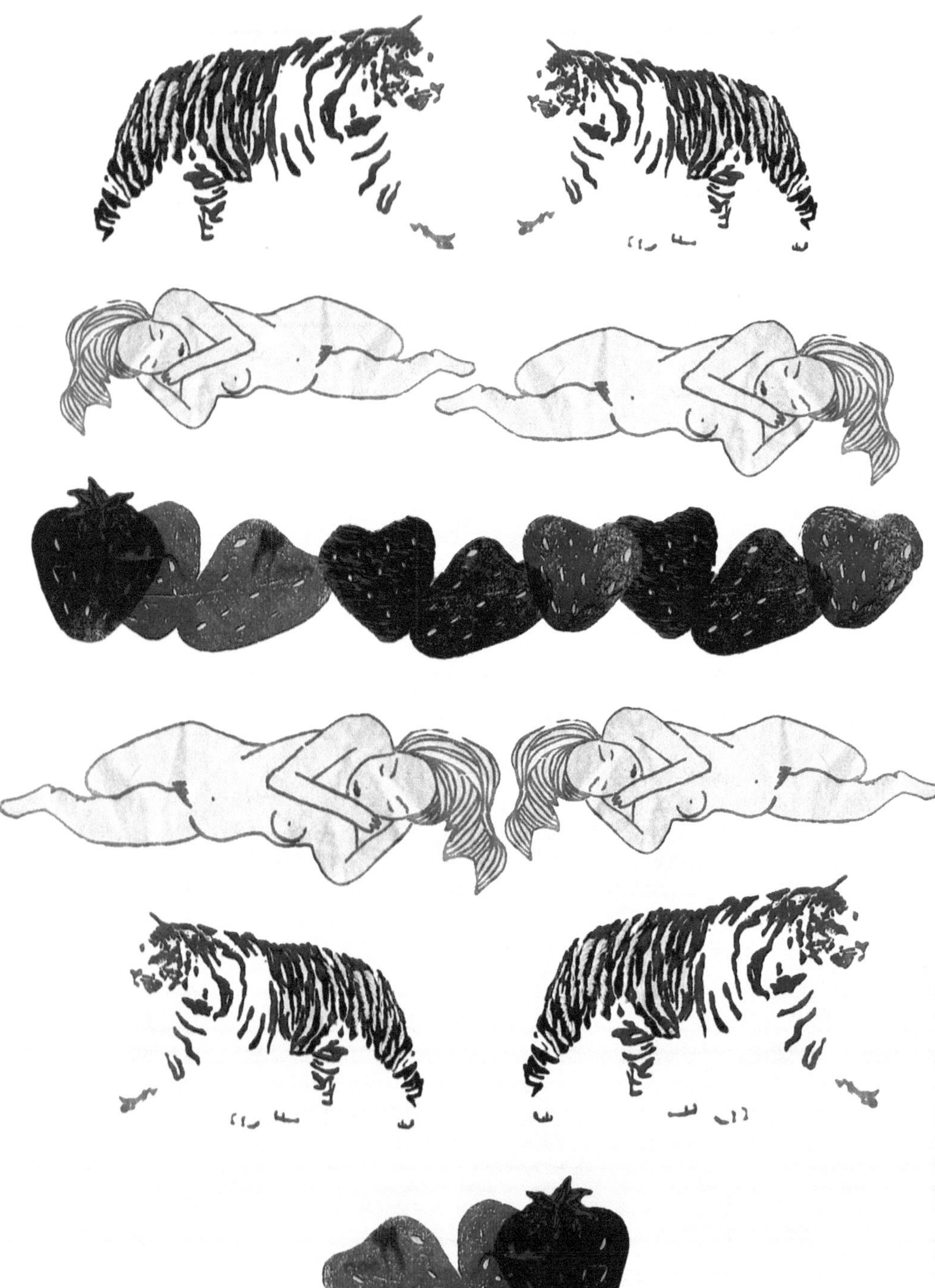

Agee in the Backyard

I could have bought my own copy of James Agee's *Let Us Now Praise Famous Men* in the past eight years—whenever I'm in a bookstore I head straight for the A's, looking for other books by James Agee there, new volumes that he came back from the grave to write. But usually there's only another copy or two of that muscular paperback, the pale green of the spine greeting me like a friend with whom I've shared countless late nights and secrets. And I always think of buying it, nine or so bucks for a used copy of my own. So I flip it open, scan the pages. And they're untouched. No creased corners or underlines like the ones my friend Meredith made during class:

> the eyes of a trapped wild animal, or of a furious angel nailed to the ground by its wings, or however else one may faintly designate the human 'soul,' that which is angry, that which is wild, that which is untamable, that which is healthful and holy, that which is competent of all advantaging within hope of human dream, that which is most marvelous and most precious…

These strange copies have no lines that I've marked, and copied and recopied into my own journals since adopting (seizing, really) the loaner.

And somehow, between the years and the pages, my own story has been seared into this volume. Within the leaves of Agee's story, another narrative is woven from photos, postcards, plane tickets, a piece of California Madrone tree bark. Vital scraps stuck between these pages—the ultimate safe-keeping place—an impeccable record is kept of where I was, who I was.

A Frida Kahlo postcard from an exhibit I attended on my twenty-third birthday in a new city on the other side of the country, anticipating the world, in which my life would begin. A letter from my sister when we lived three thousand miles away from each other: "This weather reminds me of last winter and how lucky we were to spend it together." And over the face of the first portrait in Walker Evans' series, a sticky note: a phone number of a student loan agency that keeps calling to collect coins I don't have. I've never called the number. There's a receipt from 2008: a Japanese restaurant in Seattle, a city I've never been to previously. The numbers have started to fade away, but I remember the dinner perfectly: I ate seaweed salad and sushi and stared out over the water. I had just graduated from college, was with adults and pretending to be one too. I was young enough to want to feel older. I teetered on the brink—of the world and what I would be in it. The sun set orange over the water and the warm June breeze sighed through it. I took a breath, found a home, in that.

In 1936, *Fortune* Magazine sent twenty-six-year-old journalist James Agee and photographer Walker Evans to Alabama to document the lifestyles of southern sharecroppers in the wake of FDR's New Deal. Agee arrived in Alabama as an apologetic outsider, a Southerner by birth living as a journalist in New York. In his resulting document, he recognizes the invasive nature of his work to the point of being tortured by it. He half loathed himself for the crime of writing about impoverished Southerners for the affluent Northern readers of *Fortune*. He saved some loathing for the readers of the resulting book too—we are only there to condescend from our high perches of disposable income and leisure time.

Agee names himself a spy, admits that he may be clumsy in his endeavor due to either his youth or lack of talent. But, he tells his audience, those limitations are the only reason we will survive what we're about to read. "If I were [capable], you would not go near it at all. For if you did, you would hardly bear to live." He notes that a book is far from the most effective means of narrative, and that he'd rather collect photos, cloth, cotton, earth, excrement, but "a piece of the body torn out by the roots might be more to the point."

Agee's account was ultimately rejected by *Fortune*, and his findings eventually took the shape of the four-hundred-page *Let Us Now Praise Famous Men*. It sold 600 copies upon its release in 1941. An alcoholic, Agee died of a heart attack at forty-five. He was posthumously awarded the Pulitzer Prize for his novel *A Death in the Family*, and his writing on film is credited with influencing contemporary film criticism. A *Chicago Tribune* book reviewer said of Agee, over twenty years after his death, that he was "bent on achieving magnificent goals that he was never able to define, even to himself."

Meredith lent me her copy when we shared a drafty old house that let the cold Vermont winters in through every crack, with a slanted front porch that held our bikes. Meredith and I built ourselves together, out of Saturdays at bookstores and record shops, at sticky-floored house shows and over coffee at our own kitchen table. *Let Us Now Praise Famous Men* had been assigned in her journalism class during our last semester of college.

"You need to read this," she said, and pressed it into my palm.

I was hesitant at first. What could I find in a chronicle of the Deep South during the Great Depression? My world was thousands of miles and generations removed from that bleak black-and-white moment. The book didn't cover my obsessions, which included the rebellions of Lou Reed, Joan Didion and Hunter S. Thompson's New Journalism, and the student uprisings of 1968. But once I picked it up, I was immediately awed by its power.

Agee's voice seemed at once commanding and pleading: "This is not a work of art or entertainment, nor will I assume the obligations of the artist or entertainer, but is a human effort which must require human cooperation."

This plea struck me as simultaneously brazen and humble: an artist begging to be heard and a human issuing a simple appeal for communication.

As far as rebellion was concerned, it was Agee's own, as his collaborator and friend Walker Evans noted, that was "infinitely costly and ultimately priceless."

As I read, *Famous Men* revealed itself as a sacred road map, a compass, 400-pages of runes, because I was twenty-two and looking for all of those, anything. I was an American who had spent the entirety of my adolescence with George W. Bush in office: a fake cowboy waging a forever war in the name of ever-larger cars. I had spent my college career studying in detail all the ways in which the world will end, and soon. I felt pummeled by the reactionary irony of the age. The naked sincerity of Agee's prose emerged as if from another world, one where humans could reliably hold onto a truth: *Human beings may be more and more aware of being awake, but they are still incapable of not dreaming,* he wrote.

Meredith and I had become friends the minute we met. We were both transfer students as sophomores and had each taken a year off after high school. We were both aspiring English majors and had been the youngest in our class growing up. She was from the same small New Hampshire town where I'd spent every summer as a kid. It seemed like fate that we both found a room in the same apartment through an online message board. Soon after starting classes, we both joined the college radio station and during our graveyard shifts sent the music of T. Rex echoing across the quiet campus into the empty darkness of the Vermont winter. Meredith schooled me in the New Wave cinema she'd been studying in her film class, and I made popcorn during our afternoon screenings of *Jules and Jim* or *L'Avventurra*. When I dropped everything to read ahead in *White Noise* for my post-modern literature class, I wouldn't let up until she read it too. We mixed orange juice with boxed wine and listened to Television cascading guitar openings on cold nights with the door of my room open to the little porch, slick with wet leaves. We spent weekends trying to live out the romance we'd absorbed from Godard and Truffaut. The band of boys we drank cheap beer with on Friday nights were too nice to try anything even when we wanted them to. But it didn't really matter; we had each other.

In describing his interactions with the sharecropping families, Agee employs an unlikely phrase for a man hell-bent on describing every object he encounters and experience he has: "what's the use of trying to say what I felt." With this, he seems to concede that the world continues, and we are only observers. The more audacious among us will be moved to chronicle what we've seen and tell the world what we think of it: a shout into the wind.

I recognized the terror and urgency in Agee's prose as my own when I read him: the knowledge that I was racing against my own imminent end to leave a mark, the bar of success or satisfaction with my own output residing somewhere above the clouds. Like Agee, I was bent on achieving magnificent goals I couldn't define even to myself. I couldn't be bothered with envisioning a career, but at twenty-two I believed in working toward achieving transcendence while living a life of moral righteousness. That younger self lives a million miles away from me now. And all of her goals would be handily dismissed by Agee himself as "the frightening vanity of...would-be purity." And yet, Agee's own debilitating self-doubt resonated deeply, as I would venture it does with many young people with writerly ambition: "If I had as much confidence about writing as I have intention, everything might be much easier. I feel the well-known prison walls distinctly thickening."

I wanted the narrative of my own life to be as breathless and messy as Agee's document. After graduation, I left Vermont first for California, then to Portland, then on to Michigan, Thailand,

Boston and Austin. My copy of *Famous Men* is my perennial constant, always the first thing I pack. Its presence reminds me that I have a tangible history, even though the scene and characters in my own life constantly change. Like Agee, I became a voyeur, a tourist, a restless observer. The years grew into a sticky tangle of self-doubt, late nights, cross-country moves, calls from collection agencies, boys who left me wanting, blind hope and a despair that felt like home. I found it preferable to the alternative of inertia.

While delving further into Agee's biography, I learned that he left Knoxville to attend Phillips Exeter Academy, in Exeter, New Hampshire. Agee's father had died when he was young, and his mother shipped him off early to become a man. Because of this, he was rootless, always wandering. I spent every summer on Exeter's campus for the first twenty years of my life; my father coached at the summer hockey camp there. Our family moved constantly: I'd lived in five states and twelve homes by the time I left for college. Exeter was the only constant in the life of my family. The hot nights with the fan running in whatever dorm apartment we were placed in for that mid-summer stretch, the rainy days that prohibited the beach and prompted my sister and I to hole up in the school's cavernous library to read magazines. The smells of pine and thunder and sun in the high New England summer felt like my real home. Then, I didn't know that James Agee had walked those same solemn corridors, sat in that same soft afternoon light, tasted the sweet air of the same corner of coastal New England. When I look back, I like to imagine he wandered the same trails on the edge of campus, over the river to the vast perimeters of the far fields I used to run in the evenings, where the grass was always wet and freshly cut.

It's been years since I first read *Famous Men*, and sometimes the book feels too precious to open, with its sincere prose as delicate and ancient as lace, which seems like it will crack and break if I touch it. What if I lift open the cover to find it's changed, that I can no longer find a truth in there? In the intervening years, I have grown harder. I am still here: guess I'm not too pure for this world—like Agee was. I've made compromises with myself to make money. I check Instagram too often. I've grown infinitely weary of the blustery brand of mid-century White Male Genius that Agee so expertly personified. The book is a manifesto of Agee's endless heartbreak and empathy for the white share-cropping families. He spares a few pages describing the plight of Black Alabamans of the 1930s while forgiving the "innocent" impoverished whites their racism. A glaring blind spot, based in his affinities with Southern whites and desire to protect them from the critical eye of Northerners. A reminder that no writer can tell an objective truth.

And after all those long work days, all those rent checks and regularly occurring heartbreaks, I became too busy and distracted to hold fast to Agee's declaration of the human soul, my own and those of everyone I'd met and everyone I'd never meet, as "angry, wild, untamable, healthful, holy, competent, marvelous and most precious." Once, I had fiercely believed in that fiery and sacred soul, my own, and that I would never be buried by some-thing as obscene as a gross yearly income. But I still find Agee's prose remarkable in its tenderness, and my own compassion is renewed by it. Today, like every other day, I'm buried under the news again: Another American body on the ground. Police weapons. The tears of a mother. The smirk of a congressman.

So I click 'retweet' on the more toothsome pronouncements of rage and grief I encounter.

What's the use of trying to say what I feel.

I wonder now if Agee was consumed with fear for the future of his nation, his America of the Great Depression. Or if he acknowledged the tragedies of his America as merely the usual turn of the imperial gears and saw his style of journalism as a means of disruption. Agee viewed the sharecroppers he lived with as being grossly exploited by an insidious system that had willfully consumed their humanity. Reading *Let Us Now Praise Famous Men* almost ninety years after Agee reported from Alabama, it becomes too evident that, in that long interim, America has not moved to lessen systemic oppression and poverty. Agee's sharecroppers still exist, in varied iterations: uninsured caregivers, migrant workers, single parents working multiple jobs and faced with eviction notices. Meanwhile, I have become concerned primarily, it seems, with satisfying the demands of my own debt and utility bills. I worry my senses have dulled, my blaze has been dimmed by a full-time preoccupation with economic self-preservation in a country that won't forgive me if I miss one day. So I return to Agee to remember how it feels to try for something more ambitious than covering the rent.

On a summer afternoon a few years ago in James Agee Park in Knoxville, Tennessee, I walked beneath the magnolia trees, the hot breeze my only companion. The city of Knoxville honored Agee in

2003 by dedicating the park to his memory on the street where he was born, now also named for him. The park is a tidy, deep-green city block, and I rounded it a few times, listening to the hum of August in Knoxville, imagining Agee languishing in that same song as a boy. *The whole memory of the South in its six-thousand-mile parade and flowering outlay of the facades of cities, and of the eyes in the streets of towns, and of hotels, and of the trembling heat...*

In the park, I was consumed by the power of his life and work and faced again with the question of my own. Tears sprang to my eyes. Tears for Agee's short life. Tears for the way his work meandered through my adulthood like a river? Tears over the growing chasm between my ideals and reality, that the moral commitments and artistic ambitions I could afford in youth and attempted to grasp onto proved increasingly costly as I grew older. A stone at the entrance of the park is engraved with Agee's words: "To those who in all times have sought truth and who have told it in their art or their living." The letters themselves are staid and simple, as if the sentiment behind them ever could be.

"It sounds conceited," he wrote to his mentor while in college, "but I'd do anything on earth to become a really great writer.

"That's as sincere a thing as I've ever said." He continued. "Do you see though where it leads me?"

On a summer break from college at Harvard, Agee decided to head west to work in the wheat fields of Oklahoma. "I've never worked, and greatly prefer such a job," he wrote to a friend. "I like to get drunk and will; I like to sing and learn both dirty songs and hobo ones and will."

"He couldn't limit himself; he was oceanic," said his friend. And what other way should anyone strive to be, I wonder now.

In the opening section of *Famous Men*, Agee references Beethoven's proclamation that one who understood his music could never know unhappiness again. "I believe it," he says. "And I would be a liar and a coward and one of your safe world if I should fear to say the same words of my best perception, and of my best intention."

When I reread that passage after visiting the park, I recognized in it what had sparked my tears. I had spent my adult life treading water in the murky cognitive dissonance of American late capitalism: we were allegedly bestowed the chance to accrue so much wealth that we'd never feel any pain, but everything hurt. Every day served as a reminder that the state didn't care if we financially survived a sick day or a bike accident, which seemed a benevolent fate compared to the deportations and state-sanctioned murders by police. With no god or religion to explain away the nihilistic hubris devouring my era, I adopted Agee as my prophet of sorrow and compassion, and his voice became a portal to something like grace.

But I am young; and I am young, and strong, and in good health, and I am young, and pretty to look at; and I am too young to worry, and so am I, for my mother is kind to me; and we run in the bright air like animals, and our bare feet like plants in the wholesome earth...

I slipped through the gate and out of the park.

"I finally bought my own copy. For the second time." Meredith told me a few years ago. We've known each other for two decades now, and she's more family than friend at this point. Our conversation is like a drive home through familiar wooded back roads, and Agee remains a beacon. I smile sheepishly at my blatant taking of her property. We live a country apart now, and I like to send her postcards, sometimes with quotes: "Acquaintances return books. Friends never do."

She recently visited my yard, now very far from her own. It was a warm May night like the ones we used to share together, when we might rouse friends to throw off all our clothes and ride our bikes through town naked at midnight, the delicious taste of freedom on our tongues. We didn't know then just how rarefied it was. Now we wake up early for work, pledge allegiance to the twenty-two-year-olds we were, and attempt to map lives under different constellations. But the leaves still swing in the dark with the breeze and the lilacs bloom again, like they always have.

Small wonder how pitiably we love our home, cling in her skirts at night, rejoice in her wide star-seducing smile, when every star strikes us sick with fright: do we really exist at all?

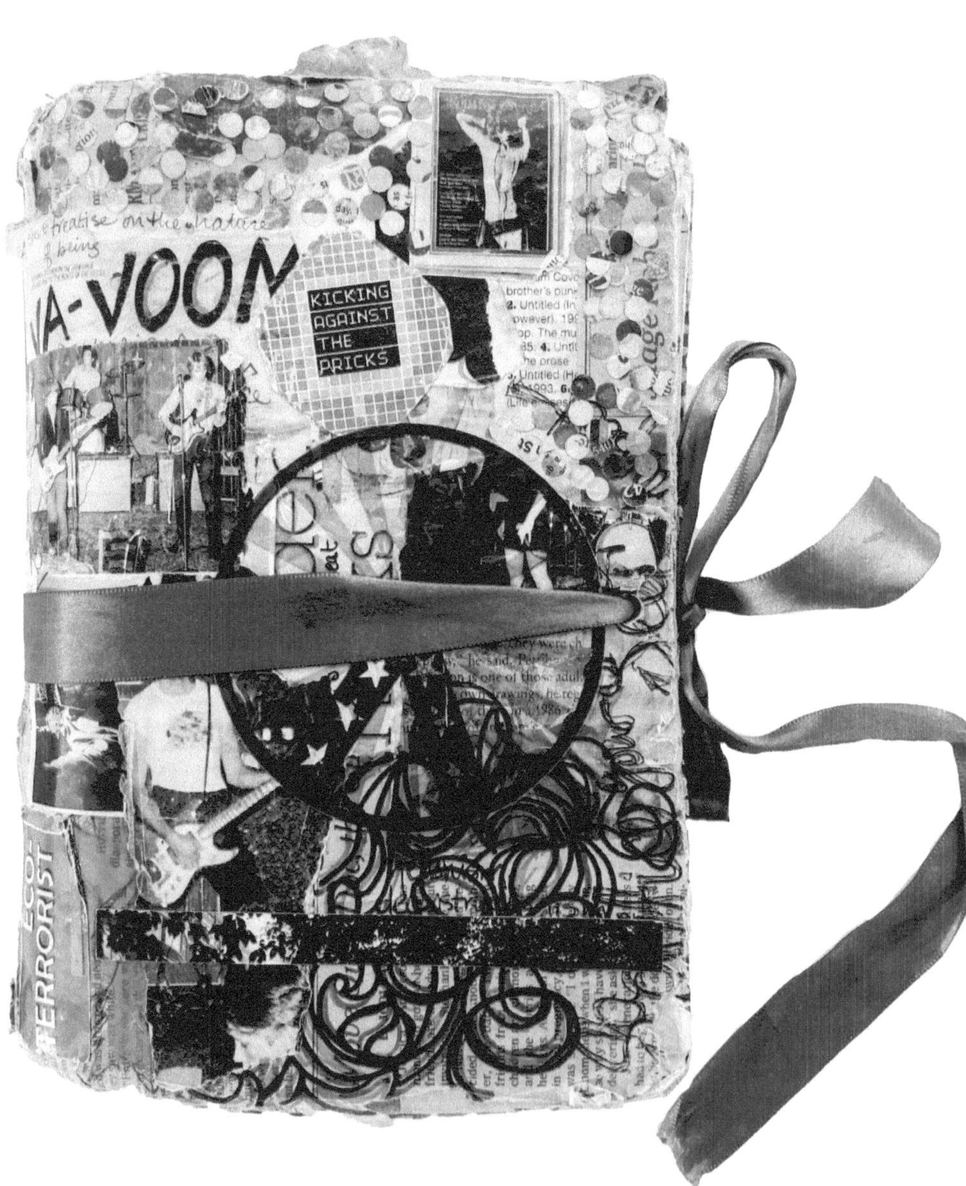
VA-VOOM
KICKING
AGAINST
THE
PRICKS
ECO-
TERRORIST

Under the Paving Stones,
the Beach!

After graduating from college, I flew out to the West Coast, looking for adventure and anything I'd never done before. I imagined that my new life in Berkeley would involve an environmental nonprofit job and sleeping with a series of handsome and alluring strangers.

"I don't really want to live in the Bay Area," my friend Kelly said when I arrived with my stack of Gary Snyder books and handsewn dresses from old T-shirts. I foisted myself on Kelly, appointed her as my West Coast tour guide. So we moved to Humboldt, where she was from, to work on a weed farm. Ten dollars an hour with room and board included.

The farm was deep in the woods, shrouded by the burning forest. We spent the days in our sports bras watering baby plants and dreaming up a poetic and pragmatic explanation of the world and how to improve it. Helicopters flew over us, attempting to see what was in the greenhouses buried in the mountains where we stood drinking lemon-lime Gatorade. DEA busts of operations like this one were in the local news daily. But we ignored that part. Our shared goal was intentionality: measured consideration of each decision that would form our lives into something singular and beautiful and ours alone. We would achieve this together.

We'd spent our last year of college sending mix CDs between Vermont and California, emailing about peak oil and boys, planning our reunion and our goal to dismantle the World Bank. I was invigorated by everything wrong with the world, and how badly it needed fixing. Kelly had all the same concerns I did: deforestation, the military-industrial complex, and making out. I liked to imagine us as a latter-day Jack Kerouac and Neal Cassady, a pair of mirrored minds that would never be satisfied by the dumb world we inhabited, reaching our full potential in tandem.

We'd secured the farm job through her high school friends. At the farm, Kelly and I talked for hours while watering the young plants and concluded that we were babies too. What was college if not a mere greenhouse? We'd studied literature and alternative energy. We could talk about DeLillo and even knew how wave power worked. I had taken a nature-drawing class the previous fall in Vermont, squinting at maples to best render their shadow and light in the low autumn sun. I could sketch a tree and its shadows pretty well. But how to live in the world, how to get what we wanted, or even to identify what we wanted: We had no idea.

The environmental studies building at my university, where I met with my advisor and brought roasted root vegetables for potluck dinners was called Bittersweet. It was as if our mentors themselves were setting us up for what lay ahead: Yes, the world is vast and beautiful and immeasurably infinite. No, you cannot access that infinity after you are gone from this place and have to earn a living.

Kelly and I wanted to travel the world, never get stuck, never sacrifice our ideals. Having to compromise what we believed in to stay alive loomed like a cliff. We wanted everything, the complete freedom to chart our own paths, but would happily settle for enough money to live.

Over the phone, I told my parents I was working on an organic farm: berries, tomatoes. On a drive, we saw a bear and her cub crossing the road in front of us. Later, when lying on a futon, I thought the shaking I felt was one of the dogs wiggling out from underneath. It was a small earthquake. So this was California. Constant raging fires, carnivorous mammals the size of Subarus, and the ground trembling underfoot.

We started each day with a joint and coffee in bowl-sized mugs and ended it with a joint and gin and tonics in the same bottomless vessels. Kelly and the boys would play guitar and sing and I'd look up at the sky, looking at the ring around the moon I'd never noticed before. At night, we watched *The Last Waltz* and watercolored, later laughing together about Neil Young from the opposite sides of the wall that separated our rooms until we fell asleep, but not before yelling "Goodnight Keh!" and "Goodnight Eh!" through the wood paneling.

One weekend, we drove down to Berkeley, Bob Dylan's *Desire* blaring through the speakers as we crossed the Bay Bridge. "She wears a necktie and a Panama hat," he warbled about some mysteriously alluring woman. We strolled Telegraph Avenue with our stacks of cash, taking it out to pay for books and Thai food. On the street, we stopped at a table dotted in turquoise and silver and both picked up rings with large stones the color of pristine oceans. Kelly's glittered robin's-egg blue flecked with black, mine aquamarine with a rust-colored halo. "Forty dollars each," said the man behind the table. "Or a homemade lasagna." We each took out two twenties and held out our hands to admire the stones. The silver settings shimmered in the sunlight.

The weekend before we left California, Kelly and I spent my birthday in San Francisco where we saw a Frida Kahlo show at the SF MOMA and ate burritos in the Mission. I had some graduation money from my parents and bought two prints from the gift shop. One was a self-portrait of Frida wearing a necklace of large blue stones, her expression both serene and determined. The other was a picnic scene: a black-and-white photo by Lee Miller of a group of friends lounging in the sun, smiling. The women are topless; one of them grins, joyful and satisfied in the company of her friends. I wanted to be a libertine too, and the scene reminded me of the afternoons I spent nature drawing. I absorbed the sun's warmth through the print. It would be a map, a blueprint for the life I would build for myself.

I slept with one of the guys at the farm, and when we left at the end of the summer, he loaned Kelly and me three thousand dollars in a Ziploc bag to start our lives in Oregon. We'd chosen Portland on a cautiously hopeful whim. Work dried up for us on the farm, or so we were told by the owner of the farm, who narrowed her eyes at us while we watered the plants in our sports bras and picked berries to make cobbler.

Upon pulling up to our new city in Kelly's red Toyota Corolla, loaded with our books, paint and thrift store boots, I made a list of my assets in my journal:

- French press
- (relatively) expensive art supplies that may or may not be used to create something worthwhile
- $1500 (spent) from an unwitting boy I wittingly slept with
- $79 (approx) in clothing
- 3 lbs organic carrots
- and something like an electric current that runs thru my veins when I am appropriately perceptive.

Kelly and I found one half of a duplex in Portland's Northeast neighborhood. A wooden swing hung from the front porch, and the backyard had patches of dry grass and a neglected compost bin in the corner. The barrier between the kitchen and living room was a waist-high wall, giving the space an open airy feel; I imagined all the parties we would host. Next to the house was an autobody shop and then MLK Boulevard, a busy north-south thoroughfare dotted with liquor stores and newer kombucha shops. Across the street, a vacant lot hosted a billboard that featured stroke awareness PSAs and Clear Channel radio station ads. It was perfect. We told our new landlord, a doctor who specialized in Eastern medicine, that we didn't have jobs yet but were interested in environmental non profit work. He handed us the keys.

Our house was a three-bedroom, two-bath, for $1650 a month. We priced the rooms by size; I took the smallest one at

$450 per month. After handing our landlord the cash for the first and last months plus security deposit, I acutely felt the clock start ticking again: thirty days to come up with another $450 and a third roommate. I painted the walls of my new bedroom a deep burgundy that I'd found in the mis-mixed pile at Sherwin Williams for three dollars. I hung the Frida Kahlo portrait next to the album sleeve of Joni Mitchell's *Blue* in large wooden frames from Goodwill. I imagined the two of them chatting with each other, and that maybe they'd teach me something. The Lee Miller print hung over my bed, a mattress and box spring from Craigslist. Kelly and I covered the hallway with postcards from our friends. We argued about what color to paint the living room: I wanted orange; she wanted something more earthy and neutral. The wall remained white.

Portland crackled with the potential energy of twenty-three-year-olds. Everyone Kelly and I met was exactly like us: early twenties, underemployed and operating within the belief that we could choose what our lives would be like and that they would be good because we had already done the hard part: we had found our way here. My optimism vibrated with a steady hum of extreme stress. But everything had worked out so far: we drove into the city with a Ziploc bag of loaned cash and convinced a landlord to let us live in his house despite having no income. Surely the hard part was over, and life was ours for the taking.

Our first week in town, we bought tickets to a music festival and spent an evening roving between downtown venues, alternating between the stage and the bar at each show. Kelly had brought a couple of weed lozenges with her from Humboldt, and we popped them halfway through the night as we watched TV on the Radio, pressed against the stage. A pleasant calm warmth coursed through my body. At the end of the night, we piled into Kelly's car to head home. We were speeding back to Northeast when a bright light came careening toward us from the left.

"Oh shit, there's a train here?" said Kelly.

It was too late to slam on the brakes, so she gunned the engine. The car flew over the tracks and landed with a heavy *ca-chunk* as the train blared its horn, missing us by what felt like inches. I gripped the door handle while my mouth gaped wide open and I turned to look at Kelly.

"Oh my god," I choked. I imagined my mom learning that I'd been killed with weed and booze in my system approximately one week into my adult life.

"Holy shit, we almost got hit by a train," she squealed, laughing and gasping. We realized we were also headed in the wrong direction. "Don't worry Eh, I'm just gonna flip around..." she said calmly, and spun the car into reverse, delivering us safely home. I knew Kelly and I could cheat death.

Kelly found a job as a barista at a French café in our neighborhood, and I cobbled together two part-time nannying positions. My savings were dwindling and I reasoned that personal checks from a mom wouldn't be held up by a two-week payroll schedule: I couldn't afford to hold out for something better or more glamorous. Kelly stole coffee from work and brought home day-old pastries, and we spent the evenings at our kitchen table collaging or painting. It felt like the beginning of something.

On early mornings in the park with the toddler I watched, I was constantly surprised to find that here a fall breeze didn't come bearing little knives of cold toward my gloveless hands. I spent my days rolling up tiny sleeves, offering her encouragement when she stood at the top of a slide, my heart stopping if she wandered too close to the edge of anything high. She pointed at birds and waved to everyone who walked past us, ecstatic to be a living thing. I tried to siphon off a little of her excitement for myself on those perfect fall days when the bright blue sky was filtered through fluorescent yellow leaves, before they corkscrewed through the air around us, settling on the ground.

In September, the stock market crashed. I had just spent four years learning mostly that we were on the brink of a great unraveling; that our world teetered tenuously on a collapsible center of fossil fuels and the consumption-based contentment of the American voting majority. It seemed clear that the contentment could turn to ire on a dime. In college, "multinational" was a slur, because it meant Dole, or United Fruit, or any company that overthrew a government to export cheap goods north, to us. I did not know what the "market" was and didn't care to; I wanted to read Gary Snyder and Allen Ginsburg under a tree on a warm afternoon and achieve communion with the universe. I wanted to meet a hot stranger and make out with him in a bar with sticky floors while loud music played.

Kelly and I spent the fall worrying on the porch swing between our work shifts. There were no jobs that could pay us enough to live, or pay for rent and groceries at the same time. "If at first you don't succeed," said a mug we'd plucked from Goodwill for the house collection, "change the rules."

We combed Craiglist for some short-term subletters for the third bedroom. A nineteen-year-old from California posted an ad that listed his passions: playing the guitar, weed and Sublime. "I wanna have a good time all the time!!!" he concluded.

"Mmmmm, no." I said. We were women of the world! We could not peacefully cohabitate with a *teenage boy.*

"Okay, you're right... but this is basically us," said Kelly, laughing.

We decided on Michael, who was moving up from the Bay Area. We listed the room, which comprised the entire top floor of the house, at $675.

"I thought you were scamming me!" he said when he arrived. "It's so cheap!"

He carried a suitcase and a cardboard cutout of Zac Ephron through the kitchen on his way upstairs. "I forgot to tell you I brought my boyfriend."

After long days spent nannying, meting out baby carrots and juice, I tried to get serious, applying to entry level jobs at environmental advocacy organizations at a maniacal clip. I was confident that the world was waiting for my ideas on how to dismantle the World Bank and ExxonMobil—or at least my relatively cheap labor. But after a while, I considered myself lucky to even receive an email regarding a part-time non profit position letting me know that *thanks, but we just had so many applicants and they all have master degrees and ten years of experience.*

The irony of chasing a toddler around for ten dollars an hour while my student loans for classes in feminist theory piled up was not lost on me. I thought of all my hours spent considering twentieth-century feminist literature—when that was my job. My professor was a Botswanan woman whose accent looped delicately around her vowels, matching the lace on the sleeves of her dresses. "Women *should* use their beauty to gain power over men!" she told us. I wasn't so sure. Now my days were spent in a haze of diaper changes and scheduling walks around naptime, and I wondered what she'd think about that. I had no power at all.

"I'm getting yellow wallpapered!!" I wailed to Kelly on our porch swing after work while we ate the day-old croissants she brought home.

"Uh, I guess," she said. "Wanna make a little dinner and watercolor?"

One weekend, I picked up an extra babysitting job. The family lived in a small house that immediately inspired me with its aspirational bohemianism. The living room was painted a vibrant deep orange and was lined with overfull bookshelves. "I love this color," I told the mom as I entered and placed my boots next to tiny sneakers on a rack in the entrance.

"It's Golden Gate Orange," she said. I swooned at this little piece of California in a Portland living room. The mother was an English professor, the father was a bartender, and the children were enrolled in a French-speaking school. The shelves in the sun-filled kitchen were tidily lined with glass jars of dried beans and pasta. The four-year-old's French coloring sheets were strewn across the kitchen table, a few crayons pulled from their yellow box.

After feeding the kids dinner, reading to them before bed and tucking them in, I tip-toed back downstairs to the living room. No TV. I scanned the bookshelves. My eye landed on *Society of the Spectacle*. In college, I'd ignored some assigned reading in favor of the school library's copy of Greil Marcus's *Lipstick Traces: A Secret History of the Twentieth Century*. Marcus details the work of the Situationists, a group of European intellectuals who sought to transcend the alienation and commodification of modern life, and I believed they had all the answers. Debord was a founding member of the Situationists, and some credit the *Society of the Spectacle* as a catalyst of the Paris uprising of May1968. Parisians plastered their city with Situationist slogans: *Neither Gods Nor Masters. The more you consume, the less you live. Under the paving stones, the beach!* Sitting in an old wooden cubicle in the school library, I'd copied these lines from Marcus's book into my journal like they were scripture.

I flipped through the pages of Debord's book. "The spectacle is the self-portrait of power in the age of power's totalitarian rule over the conditions of existence." *Well, sure*, I thought. I copied it into my journal. I couldn't wait to chat about it with Kelly when I got home, over a beer. "The more readily [the spectator] recognizes his own need in the images of need proposed by the dominant system, the less he understands his own existence and his own desires.... The spectator feels at home nowhere, for the spectacle is everywhere."

So we were all alienated from existence and the material conditions that surrounded us. Okay. But when did the pre-spectacle era occur, and why was I stuck here, babysitting on a Saturday night to be able to eat, in a society that had labeled my value a net-negative? When did the modern conditions of the spectacle and alienation begin? Would I have been freer to achieve self-actualization as a serf in medieval times, or at any point in history when I would have had no option but to begin procreating as early and as often as possible, and likely die in the process?

I left the Golden Gate living room that night with sixty bucks in cash: a small fortune. I should have gone grocery shopping, but the next day I went to the Portland Book Fair instead, and bought an art book by Lawrence Weschler. It illustrated the uncanny overlapping of reality and art, images from our contemporary world replicating classic paintings in an inexplicable symmetry, looping through each other and back again to create a third, secret truth for those who could see it. A Rothko as the moon landing. A landscape as a Velasquez Venus. I wondered which piece of art would reflect my reality, what could I hold up and match to my world like a twin.

"Dude, we're so fucked," said Kelly. "Everyone is just like horny for Daddy McCain to bomb the middle east off the map."

We were at the neighborhood bar with our new friend Lilly on a warm night, drinking eight-dollar cocktails we couldn't really afford. The election was two months away.

"Yeah, because everyone in this country is dumb. Maybe we need like a benevolent dictator to just tell us what to do," Lilly said.

I slurped on my cocktail. "We should make merch that's like 'the economy collapsed and all I got was drunk,'" I said.

In that moment, the lives we'd been planning for, the world we'd taken out untold sums of money to propel ourselves into, no longer existed. It was terrifying yet somehow predictable. How childish, how *middle-class*, to think we could wriggle free of the gnashing teeth of the American economy and achieve satisfaction and toplessness in the sun. A sunny patio and credit to absorb the cost of our cocktails helped soften the blow. We would laugh and toast to nothing and smash our empty glasses down, just like Joni.

Everyone around us at the bar was extremely hot. In Portland, everyone was hot. I was always trying to catch the eye of the bar's silent bearded door guy. He was usually reading Richard Brautigan. Inside, I learned that any man you hope will come up and talk to you because he looks cute and nice and knows how to read never will, because that's not what thoughtful men do.

But mostly I was in love with the city itself: its slick streets, purple sky, and everyone who could always hang out because they barely worked. I began my days when the mornings were still gray, riding my bike through the wet leaves to the train, which I rode to the suburbs for my nannying job. The fall air was warm and humid, the light mist in my eyelashes so foreign: how did I make it out here, to a rain forest?

After work, I met up with my even less-employed friends for cheap beer and a free show. "Two-dollar drafts at East Burn," my phone would light up reliably in the late afternoon. There was always a show. "We're at the Know, free show at nine." Around the city, there was a lot of art that involved human bodies and animal heads, mostly with antlers, as if we had all agreed that being human was less than noble and would trade it in given the chance.

At the end of the night, I'd ride my bike northward home, letting go of the handlebars and steering with only a slight, knowing shift of my weight, hands in pockets, daring myself. Rolling past the bread factory on 11th Street, I breathed in its comforting warmth. My front bike light ricocheted like a strobe off of the stop signs I carelessly rolled through. The mist dotted my nose, pooling into droplets that dripped into my mouth. The air passing through my lungs and out again into the night, as my legs rhythmically propelled the bike ever forward, felt like a poem thrummed out to the beat of my quickened pulse.

"Indulge untrammeled desire," I scribbled some late night, another Situationist slogan forever lighting up the inside of my mind.

On nights we stayed in, we sat at our kitchen table, collaging and drinking beer, our door open to whomever wanted to join us. On weekends we hosted parties, the house filled with people we knew and people we'd never seen before. Red wine was spilled on the carpet; someone broke someone's new bong. Every Sunday, Lilly hosted "no pants crazy hat" potlucks. After arriving in her doorway carrying a six-pack or a salad, we unzipped and wiggled out of our jeans, and chose a hat from a large cardboard box she kept on a bench under the coat rack. Lilly turned up the Van Morrison, and conversation turned to the election, shows we'd been to, annoying bosses or customers at work. We all were either without jobs to wake up for on Monday or too young to ever have hangovers, and the fifteen of us drank red wine until our teeth were purple and danced in the dining room. That's what I had come here for.

Guiding my tires through the decomposing leaves—as they made their way back into the ground in the fall, and under the new bursts of blooms in the spring—felt to me like being born. Portland was its own universe, and it seemed like everything that mattered was happening within the city's grid. The rules of American adulthood were being rewritten here into something less dismal. We did not wear make-up, have our hair cut professionally or ever wear clothes that hadn't belonged to someone else first. At the time, I felt there was an implicit purity in that, a divestment from whatever anxiety-riddled, reality-show-addicted spectacle America was trying to buy its way into. Here, there was an air of discovery, of adventure—that everyone in the bar or café or at the show could be a friend or someone to fall in love with if you just ended up talking, that maybe great art or a new way of living was being invented here, now. I believed that we had the ability to rewrite the rules, to create the world we wanted. Maybe all of that was an illusion, maybe none of that was real for anyone else. But to me, for a short time, the whole city was alive with that belief.

After so many late nights and searching for their toll on my face in the morning, I decided I would probably be a straight-edge Buddhist by thirty. It was the oldest I could imagine a person, or at least myself, being. I imagined that at thirty, I would not *want* anything; I would have achieved enlightenment by then. For now, I always wanted more: the music to be louder, to stay up a little later. I lived by a line I picked up from James Agee: "A little too much is just enough for me."

As much as I longed for a certain level of stability, I was invigorated by the freedom of being adrift, relaying the events of my life in stark bullet points to my parents on the phone from the other side of the country. Chasing men who didn't want me and ignoring the ones who did, belonging to no one: it gave me something to write about. I made journals by binding overdue utility bills from Pacific Power and notices of my defaulted student loans into record covers with satin ribbon, and I filled them with scribbled notes about boys who were distracting enough to memorialize there, among lines from books that would ultimately construct my permanent home: "*I dedicate myself to the universal diamond—be this raging fury destroyed*–Gary Snyder." Jay Cantor: "*I understood: capitalism: a top-hatted magician turning dead people into round gold coins.*"

By Christmas, I needed a new job. One of the moms from a family I nannied for had been laid off and no longer needed me. The other family was moving to California. After submitting around one hundred job applications through idealist.org, I secured a spot in a group interview for an hourly position at a study abroad organization. I wore my most professional outfit: a plum-colored button-down shirt from the boys' section at Goodwill over a black T-shirt dress I'd made, and silver beads that my grandmother had given me. I brushed my dark curls back and pinned them in what I hoped was a responsible manner and rode the train to the downtown office on a weeknight. There were twelve of us seated around a large table: a coliseum of sorts, in which we all had to fight each other for the attention of our overlords as they dangled the prize of ten dollars an hour in front of us. The stakes having been established as the ability to continue to pay the rent, I wedged myself into the conversation as much as I could.

It worked: I was hired along with the two other people who talked the most during the interview. The position was "Assistant

Advisor," which meant that Sunday through Thursday from 12 to 8 pm we made our way through a database of names of high-school students all over the country who had expressed interest in traveling abroad for a semester. Our job was to call them, remind them they wanted to go to Japan and ask if they were still interested. To avoid providing us benefits, the organization classified assistant advisors as "full-time temporary," brought on for six months for thirty-five hours a week (lunch was not paid). I might not have a job by July, but for now I could keep Frida and Joni comfortably housed in my burgundy bedroom.

During our shift, five of us sat in a row, our computer monitors lined against the bright white wall, drenched in fluorescent light. We were tasked with registering Skype accounts; I chose the name "partie.tyme." I began each work day crossing the Broadway Bridge with a caravan of other cyclists, silently regarding my compatriots as if we were part of something together, or at least avoiding sitting in traffic. Riding over the bridge, I felt a little bit free.

At work, I spent most of the day reading the internet, blogging about shows I went to and the importance of eco-terrorism, and g-chatting my friends. I wondered if the internet was invented just so people would have something to do at work.

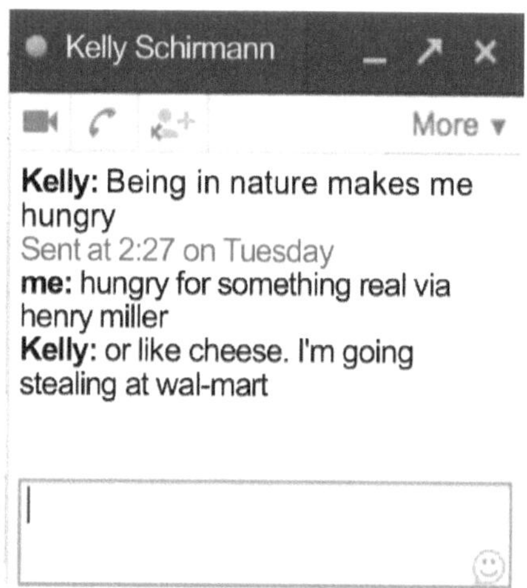

Sometimes I'd g-chat my coworker at the computer next to me. Brian was my age, a black-haired skater from San Diego in tight jeans who went to house shows every night and came in hungover every day.

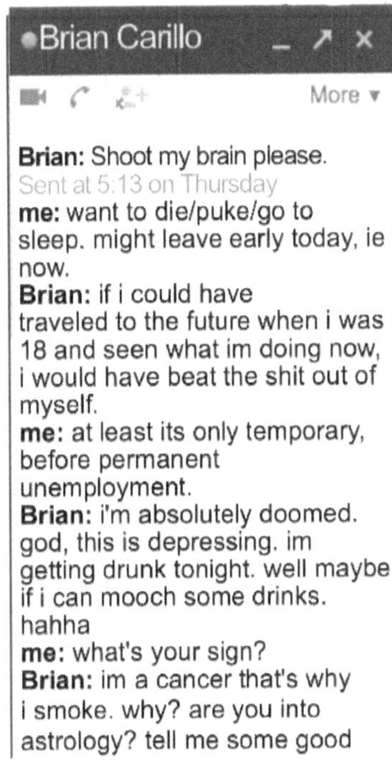

Occasionally, I would pick up the phone and do my job.

"Hi, this is Emily calling for Chris... he expressed interest in studying abroad?"

"This is his dad. Which broad? Heh."

".....well... he said he's interested in Spain? But... actually we have Spanish language programs in multiple Latin American countries."

There was a food truck park near the office, and after the lunch rush, the gourmet pizza truck would sell the remaining slices on clearance: two for five bucks. I'd take a late lunch and get two slices of pizza, which also covered dinner. Sometimes, on payday when I felt flush, I'd walk up to the landmark coffee shop, and share over-long, over-obvious eye contact over my cappuccino with the hot barista, the glossy whole-milk froth a thick luxury. On rainy days, I took the light rail downtown to work instead of biking, skipping the two-dollar ticket fee and quickly jumping off if I saw a MAX employee circling the train car checking tickets.

five years unhappy labor/22 to 27 working/ not a dime in the bank/ to show for it anyway: Allen Ginsberg echoed in my brain.

My office had a color copier, and the regular full-time staff was gone by six. I pasted together a Situationist-inspired zine from pages of *National Geographic*, my overdue student loan statements and phrases I'd typed on an old typewriter I picked up for five bucks. I called it "I wanna have a good time all the time!!!" and ran the pages through the work copier in the dark office. *We all practice our own secret anarchies*, I wrote.

On days when I wanted something new but couldn't afford anything, I would visit the library and leave with a tall stack of books I'd never read before. I favored biographies about musicians who had constructed something out of nothing, sometimes going on to live in glamourous excess in Laurel Canyon. I aspired to both. *We must for dear life make our own counter-realities*, went a Henry James line I copied into my journal.

One day, I would be very far from here, but I would remember it all, especially biking over the bridge, the sun low in the purpling sky as I headed home to Northeast, a small corner of a city that I loved, in a country that rarely made sense to me. "We will do every thing we set out to," I wrote during that time, a command to myself. "We have to."

"Morning, bitch," said Michael as he made his way into the kitchen in his red and black checkered lumberjack nightie. He took out the coffee grinder. "Want some?" He hadn't found a job and was usually busy watching *Sex and the City,* on DVDs he checked out from the library, while drinking a bottle of André. He'd started referring to the *Sex and the City* characters as his friends, and it wasn't uncommon to get updates on what Charlotte or Samantha were up to in New York. He was running low on his savings and had recently taken to selling his belongings on Craigslist. His plunger had brought in two dollars. Even Zac Ephron had to go: for fifteen bucks to the host mom of a German exchange student. That morning over coffee, I opened the quarterly water bill: It was $200. My pulse quickened. Every time I received one, it would derail me for the rest of the month. I'd charged Kelly and Michael monthly for the bill, with the intent to have the money ready when the bill came. Instead, I'd promptly spent their contributions and now had to pony up the two hundred myself.

After I wrote a check and licked the envelope, I realized I had fifty dollars to last until my next paycheck in two weeks. I took my coffee into my bedroom and rooted around for any stray bills that might be lingering in the pockets of my jeans. All that greeted me was the sound of the mice in my closet, chomping away loudly on the piles of overdue student loan notices I'd thrown in there. At least the mice were eating well. I hadn't had a salad in months. I'd been living on caffeine, pastries and beer. I felt a familiar stomach lurch over my pathetic station in life.

My phone buzzed: it was Lilly, calling to see if I wanted to go to brunch. Of course I did, and promptly spent half my net worth on an omelet. When I arrived home from work, I realized the refrigerator was nearly empty and snacked on a leftover scone Kelly had brought home. The next morning, I re-steeped the coffee grounds from the day before; we were out of coffee. "I would run the caffeine under my fingernails through a French press right now!" said Michael.

That day, I received a package from my mom: a bottle of vitamins, a box of granola bars and a ten-dollar bill. "Thinking of you... just like a mom to wonder: Are you getting enough iron? Love ya, Mom."

After six months at the study abroad office, my hours were cut to 19 per week and I was now classified as "part-time permanent": still no benefits. In August, there was a stretch of days over one hundred degrees, the hottest weather I'd ever experienced, without the afternoon New England thunderstorms to puncture the fever dream. When I left the office at 8 pm, the heat visibly emanated off of anything metal in thick waves. Riding my bike home felt like traversing the surface of the sun, and at home I filled up the bathtub with cold water, ate a popsicle if the neighborhood ice cream truck was rolling past the house, and pretended I was in a pool until I felt reanimated.

On my new abbreviated work schedule, I was making $800 per month. Michael had just applied to a barista position that had garnered 200 applicants, and I didn't have the energy for another round of job applications. I did have the energy to exorcise my constant stress and misery onto some scavenged print media. After work, over a dinner of a 22-ounce beer and snack-sized bag of Smartfood, I pounded out phrases on my typewriter and glued them onto images from old *National Geographic* magazines. "Globalized capitalism is a bad idea!" over a photo of kittens, "part-time revolutionaries unite!" on a group relaxing on a boat in the 70s. "I'm gonna marry the next dude I meet who's not in a band" on an 80s black-and-white photo of a punk. "Religion and politics are unnecessary to the culture who has poetry" a quote I picked up somewhere, pasted onto a woman in a bikini, lounging in a beach chair. "Portland, OR: lots of booze and no sense of urgency" over an orange and purple gradient of a city sunset.

I glued them to flat rectangle magnets, trotted them out to the monthly art walk in my neighborhood, and sold them to people from all over the city who laughed when they picked them up. It felt like making my own counter-reality, for dear life.

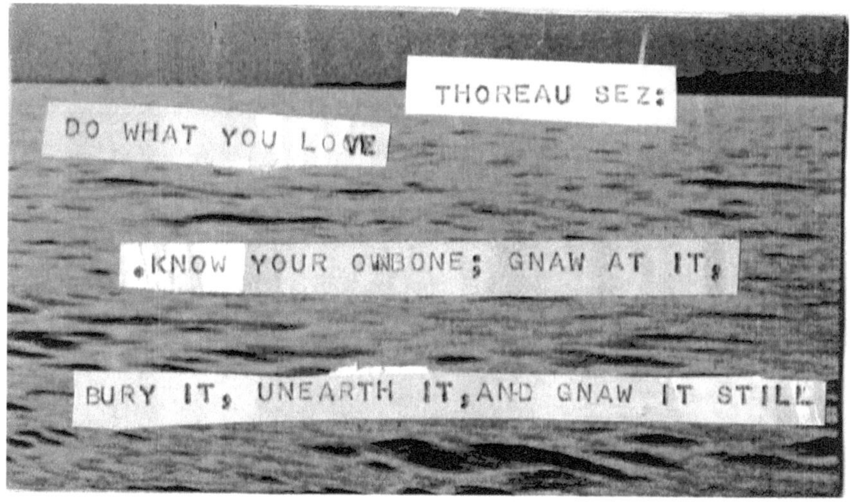

I kept one of my favorite magnets for myself: Thoreau's dictum "Do what you love. Know your own bone; gnaw at it, bury it, unearth it, gnaw it still." I placed it on the fridge, where it taunted me every morning before I rode my bike to work, invariably got rained on, and cried at my desk over my failure to achieve my dreams, or to be able to afford fresh produce. I didn't even have time to sing the body electric.

I set out to live a life of constant discovery and receptivity to the world around me, to escape the misery of American adulthood and create something meaningful. Like any idiot. Was regularly crying at my desk at work a nervous breakdown, or was this a rite of passage, my soft flesh and ideals being forged by the fire of low pay and debt into my final form: the deadening acceptance that art and joy do not belong in this world? Was this just the spectacle succeeding in its cruel but certain work? I wrote in my journal, "The real fear is existing in a world that regulates experience thru money, and having a lot of life to live but not enough money to live it." The truth of being twenty-three, perhaps, is realizing everything for the first time and believing that no one else ever has before.

On the way to work one day, I flew off my bike, over the handle bars, and landed on my head. One thought reverberated through my most elemental unconscious chambers while I was in mid-air: *"I can't afford this."* My helmet sustained a crack: The white plastic cleft neatly in two like a relief map rendering of an earthquake. That night, I rode my bike to a free community health clinic near my house to make sure I wasn't terminally concussed. The clinic was crowded; I found a seat outside on the porch and filled out a stack of forms. A woman on the bench across from me in a T-shirt that insisted *America!* talked loudly into her cell phone.

The sky was clear for the first time in weeks; the full moon hung serenely above us. "I'm just happy y'all are here," said a woman near me to the nurse who collected her paperwork. "Hopefully one day we'll all have healthcare," she replied.

"Maybe Obama will make it happen," I offered, and the woman smiled at me.

"He's got the weight of the world on his shoulders," said the nurse.

In the hallway, Mary Ann, RN, took my blood pressure. "Beautiful. That's only possible when you're ...23," she said, glancing at my form. The nurses, with their short hair and glasses, tapered jeans, comfortable shoes and genuine kindness, were unmistakably motherly; I was tempted to crumple before them, as they would calm, and assure, and fix me. My own sense of personal and professional despair that ruins us all was slowly ruining me. That is, the fear that it doesn't matter what we make, that we were wrong to ever think it would, and that our only purpose in this world is to consume plastic items made to break too soon, to buy something large, lots of large things, and spend the rest of our lives working to pay them off. I was rattled so thoroughly by my financial responsibilities and my inability to meet them that I could barely know my own bone, let alone gnaw it.

I didn't know then that longing is a perpetual state.

Mary Ann told me that I might have a slight concussion, but nothing too serious, although I shouldn't land on my head again because then my brain might bleed. I thanked her, hopped on my bike and looked up at the full moon. I rode fast enough to feel the night breathing on me, through me, trying to free myself from the constant stress and fear of not being able to afford an existence without giving in to a life of extracting natural resources from a developing country or working for some cheerfully branded entity that was actually contracting with the department of defense.

I rode north to the karaoke bar where Lilly and Michael were flipping through a heavy white binder of songs. "Welcome, bitch. You're alive!" said Michael, handing me an empty glass and a pitcher of Pabst Blue Ribbon. Lilly and I scanned the binder while Michael got onstage and performed a raucous rendition of George Michael's "Father Figure." He ended on his knees, sliding across the waxed dancefloor.

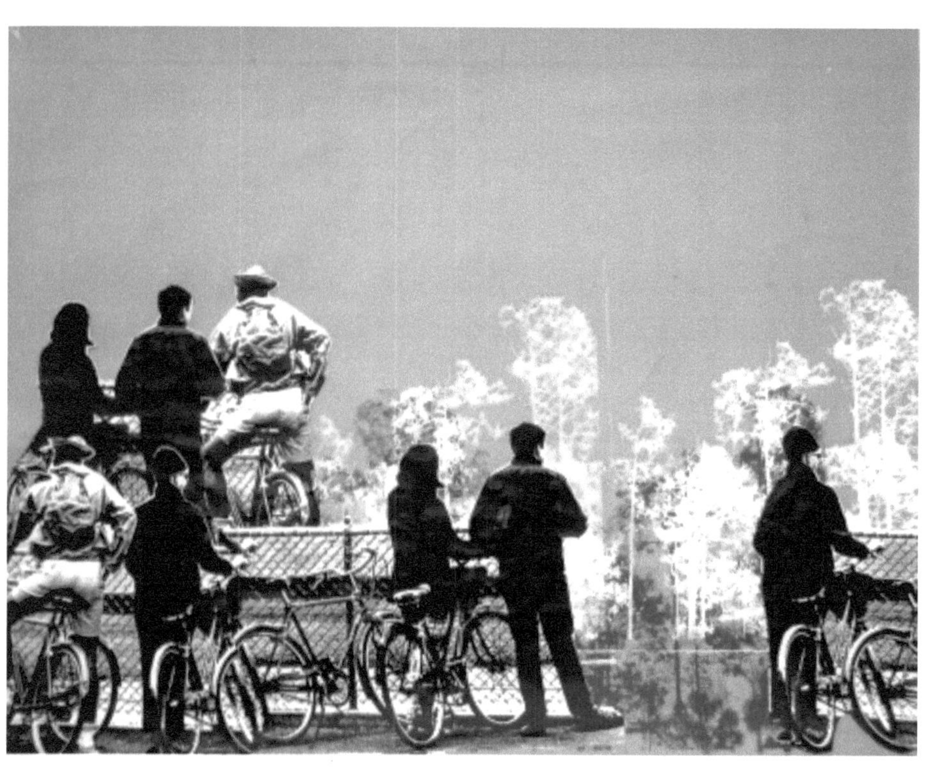

Your Freedom Country

October in Bangkok is hot and rainy. I stared out into the city from the back of a pink cab in gridlock, the windows streaked with my own breath. I'd arrived in the capital after a ten-hour bus ride. I had twelve hours to kill as I waited for another bus to take me farther south, to the beach where my friends awaited. While in Bangkok, I was headed to a place called Siam Paragon, at the recommendation of a Thai friend. I had no idea what this Paragon was, but luckily the cab driver understood my stilted Thai.

I had spent the previous six months teaching English to high schoolers in northeastern Thailand. My placement was in Roi Et, a province in Isaan, the nation's largest, poorest and most rural region. When I told the cab driver in Bangkok where I'd been living, he laughed and asked "Roi Et? Why?!" as if I were a visitor to America on a layover in New York, bound for Topeka. When I arrived, I spotted few other foreigners in my new town, all of them middle-aged, male and European. *Falangs*.

I arrived in Thailand at twenty-four on a scholarship with a group of seventeen other American teachers. We were looking for adventure or maybe purpose, because we believed we deserved it. We decided to try our luck in a place with a completely different alphabet while earning two hundred American dollars a month. I boarded the plane with a head full of development theory, Allen Ginsberg's poems in my suitcase, a homemade haircut and a thrift store jacket. I was going as far as possible from where I was because I was afraid that if I stayed in one place too long, the ground would turn to cement, my feet would sink in, and I would miss out on the life I was meant to live, the life that was happening everywhere else. By twenty-four, I had already moved across the country twice on my own and lived in England and Belize.

"I just wanted to know the world, see what it felt like." I wrote in my journal on the flight to Bangkok.

The day before I began my teaching assignment at Muang Suang Wittaya, my advisor, P'Duong, brought me to the tallest standing Buddha statue in Thailand: Roi Et's greatest attraction. Outside the temple, P'Duong handed me a small bouquet of yellow flowers, two yellow candles and some incense.

"For success," she said, and we lit the candles and incense and set them on the altar.

The next day in the classroom, I was in desperate need of *any* charms for success. Turned loose in front of a classroom of 30 Thai teenagers, I made up the lesson plan in a few seconds with my back turned toward the white board. The desks were crammed together; a fan whirred in the back of the classroom as the sun glared white hot. In a flash of inspiration, or desperation, I remembered the World Cup was happening. After I introduced myself, I called on each student to come to the front of the room and say "My favorite team is _____." But first, they had to shake my hand, American style. Not a student could conceal their mortification. I smiled and their friends laughed as each of them haltingly read "My. Favorite. Team is. Bra. ZEEL," off the white board.

My official duty was volunteering; my fellow teachers and I were provided a small stipend of about two hundred American dollars a month from our schools, plus a bonus of six hundred dollars from the Thai government at the end of the term. Even inexperienced English teachers from the West are paid up to twice what veteran Thai English teachers earn; volunteers in my program were placed at schools unable to afford the hefty foreigner salary. In a bid to enter the final phase of development, Thailand had decided that English would become their official second language, and we were there to help them reach that goal.

On the other side of the world, the sunlight was different. Brighter, whiter. And I was strange in it, an alien to everyone around me. "You look like Lady Gaga," my new friend's little sister told me. Suddenly, my nose is lovely. Why am I not blonde, and why are my eyebrows black: Are both of my parents *really* American? I'm "big" or "soft" or "slender," depending on the day. My tan is *not* beautiful. I started to feel like Lady Gaga because everyone wanted a photo with me. My host mother christened me with the nickname *Champu*, the name of a flower, and also meaning "pink": the color of my cheeks in the relentless warmth. "Crickets. Heat. Heat and crickets and heat," I wrote in my journal.

Another English teacher, P'Vee, brought me a coconut snack wrapped in a palm leaf every morning. The English department at my school gifted me with a few yards of raw Thai silk, to be sewn by a tailor into traditional garments that the teachers wore to school each Wednesday. The silk was a bright turquoise. "Blue for Champu!" said P'Duong, smiling as she placed it in my hands.

As my taxi approached Siam Paragon, I understood why my well-meaning friend had thought I would want to visit. The line to get into a newly-opened Krispy Kreme shop snaked around the massive, Western-style shopping center, which billed itself as "the Jewel of Bangkok." Wat Pho, the eighteenth-century temple, encrusted in gems and home to a 150-foot reclining golden Buddha, its feet inlaid with pearl, sat just across the city.

The American teachers I was on my way to meet were already busy sipping mango smoothies on the beach, snorkeling and probably sleeping with athletic Germans. In Siam Paragon, I spent the afternoon wandering the white marble floors, past shops selling Dior sunglasses and a Lamborghini showroom. In the food court, Europeans barked out orders for bagels. I'd been staring at the reflection of the sun in a flooded rice field for months, and here in the mall, the garish neon lights on the waxed and buffed floors quickly shook me awake, back into a world constructed solely of items for sale, the world I was from. Here I was an alien even to myself, a ghost floating through the wide halls, searching for a long enough English-language novel for my ten-hour bus ride. I'd spent my tweenhood in malls: every Friday night with my friends, spending my babysitting money on a new color of nail polish, the current issue of *Seventeen Magazine*, and an Auntie Anne's pretzel. I'd make a call to my parents from the payphone when it was time be picked up. And here, on the other side of the world, I found another mall.

In Roi Et, I lived on sticky rice and a hybrid of Thai-English that left plenty of room for miscommunication. At school, P'Duong said that I should be teaching the students about America. But I'd planned to avoid the topic of America altogether, as my presence alone already implied more in the way of cultural hegemony than I was comfortable with. So I focused on relaying the finer points of English slang and weather jargon to the students as they slouched in their chairs and closed their eyes, bored out of their minds. It wasn't until I made flashcards from an issue of *Rolling Stone* that my friend Molly in Austin had sent me that it became clear that what the students really wanted to know about was America. Movie star, rock star, guitar. I held up an ad for Twilight, intending to prompt "movie," but they all squealed "Edward!" Now I was getting somewhere. I held up a photo of Obama, for "president." Neighboring Indonesia claims him as one of their own, making him Thailand's cousin. My class of thirty shouted "o-ba-MA!"

The school's music teacher was Mr. Jojo; He was compact with an angular face and copper skin and parted his shiny black hair to the side. I'd first seen him early in the semeste, in a black T-shirt and jeans. I thought he looked cool, a playful and brooding James Dean or Gael Garcia Bernal. I told my friends Katae and Fai I thought he was cute, and they shrieked with excitement. Thais like to say that gossip is their national sport, and all the young teachers at the school started pushing us together; we stumbled through some conversations, smiling. Somehow, I talked to his parents on the phone, all of us laughing through my basic Thai and their collection of English words. "Champu! You like Jojo?" They asked me. "Ka, chop mak," I laughed. *I like him lot.*

Despite trying to appear somewhat teacherly to the teenagers in my classes and aid in their learning any English at all, I didn't have an interest in being respectable all the time. I crave a little chaos. The week before leaving for my beach vacation, the school hosted an end-of-semester party. I sat with Katae and Fai in the gym on folding chairs at a round table with a floral tablecloth where my Johnny Walker and soda glass remained consistently filled. Katae, Fai and I cheered on the other teachers as they took turns singing ballads on the karaoke stage.

At the party, Jojo and I danced, approximating something like a tango; I ended up with a carnation in my teeth, and swirled my red skirt around until it fanned out like a flower in full bloom. Thai pop was mixed in with Western classics; "Hotel California" made its routine appearance. Toward the end of the night, I dragged him outside the gym and our mouths found each other. As soon as it began, Fai materialized to pull us apart. She spoke sharply to Jojo and hit him on the arm like he was a misbehaving dog: a pin in the bubble of my whiskey dream. Fai led me back into the gym while I tried to smile behind my shoulder at Jojo. The crickets and heat pulsed. I straightened my skirt, went back to dancing and tried not to think about the fact that I had just torn through the fine mesh of the social fabric, bringing shame to myself, Mr. Jojo and his family, and the entire Western world by being a feckless slut.

I spent the night at Fai's house and cried, drunk and knowing I had done something wrong. We were in our pajamas, sitting on her living room floor as the TV played in the background. "Don't be a water face," Fai said, handing me a tissue. "Falang are free," she explained to me slowly. "Thai people are... not so free."

I spent the weekend moderately concerned that I'd be blacklisted at school on Monday, with a scarlet letter tattooed on my forehead, my indiscretions recounted in detail over and over to each member of the faculty. I wondered what P'Duong, who never had a hair out of place and could scare a roomful of rowdy students into submission despite being extremely tiny, would think of me. But the only reaction that I received out of the norm on Monday was a heartier greeting than usual from the assistant principal, a jolly woman who liked to laughingly note that we were united in our shared burden of large busts, and had cheerfully responded "Good, good!" when I'd asked for a beer at the party.

I wondered if my transgression was so grave that Fai had told no one, in order to protect me. Previously, whenever Jojo would bring me an iced tea, my friends would egg me on for a week, joking that we would get married. After the party, Fai and my other friends at school never mentioned Jojo to me again.

On my afternoon in Siam Paragon, an American movie seemed like the perfect indulgence. I found the cinema, emptied a can of Singha down my throat in the lobby and took a seat in the dark empty theater. A short clip filled the screen: a montage of the King of Thailand as a young man, dutifully dirtying his hands with farmers in the countryside, then decorated regally, solemnly flanked by the rest of the royal family. It was a standard government-issued reel assigning Thailand's wealth, good fortune and transition to modernity to the beloved long-ruling monarch.

The national anthem began. I glanced around: The six other people in the theater–the type of white-haired, khaki-d men I'd seen wandering the red-light districts of tourist towns–were on their feet. I jumped up to join them as a warning from an orientation instructor from my group's first week in Thailand echoed in my mind. She informed us that anyone who opposes or disrespects the king could be thrown in jail: "This is not your freedom country."

It had only been a couple of years since the crash of 2008 that had rendered most of my generation disillusioned, listless and underemployed. Major news outlets liked to wonder why we weren't buying houses and blamed us for a slow economic recovery. What was I supposed to do, take out 80 thousand in loans to ride out the recession in grad school? I'd spent undergrad writing about art for the college paper, hosting a radio show, considering nature versus culture and believing that those things mattered. And I would pay for it for the rest of my life. There were no jobs; my "freedom country" felt more like a cratered dead-end. So I used the teaching scholarship I was awarded at twenty-four and the Western native-English-speaking privilege I was awarded at birth to fly to Thailand, and now I sat alone in a movie theater half a world from home, happy to absorb the dumb luster of Hollywood fantasy reflecting off my retinas for an afternoon.

Oliver Stone's unwitting paean to the craven Wall Street excesses of the 80's through the figure of Gordon Gekko begat a sequel based on the financial collapse of 2008. *Wall Street II: Money Never Sleeps* was the perfect choice for this hot afternoon: I could shake my head at the hubris of my nation from the other side of the world. I could be rueful from this distance. The film belongs to a genre that feels kind of like homework: We have to know what derivatives or corn futures are, or understand what shorting a market means. We can be mad at the villains, and the frayed political anxieties of our age are smoothed, molded and projected onto a screen large enough to contain them, if only for ninety minutes. Our collective ire is temporarily vindicated, perhaps even mollified by a director whose politics we sort of share.

The previews rolled for a slew of Japanese and Korean action films, sparser in military-porn and explosions than the usual Hollywood-minted sequel or remake, but making up the difference with hand-to-hand combat. Quick cuts between bombs, bras and the obligatory slow-mo shooting spree comprised the majority of the clips. Alone in my seat in this dark theater, I wondered if America's most significant export is the expensive slick and breathless glamour of cartoon violence. More likely, all of humanity is united in our thirst for it, and America just built the biggest studios.

In my high school US History class, we watched *Platoon*, Stone's 1986 best-picture Academy Award winner. I'm not sure why we watched it; I don't remember studying the Vietnam war. My teacher was twenty-five and usually stoned or hungover during class, but he swam at Yale so it was fine. *Platoon* aims to expose the damage war inflicts not only on the killed but also on the killers, the dehumanization inherent in becoming a brutalizer as well as the terror in being brutalized. *Aren't we all haunted by the human condition, man?* But as I sat in our classroom and absorbed the glee with which the American soldiers attack the Vietnamese men, women, and children, it seemed as if the camera itself was enthralled with this violence, with no real ability to condemn it. The bloodthirstiness in the frame made me feel sick. Pauline Kael called it "too damn much romanticized insanity." The film was critically lauded overall as the best film of the year despite a groan-inducing voiceover from Charlie Sheen as Chris, the American naïf: "We weren't fighting the enemy; we were fighting ourselves." This seems to hint at Americans' collective desire to view ourselves as uniquely complicated: entitled to violent dominion, but tortured about it so ultimately noble. But what the movie proves is that Americans really want is to a watch Americans bashing in non-American skulls. Even in a movie purported to critique this violence, the muscle of American power glistens with Vietnamese blood, and I realized that anti-war cinema is a lie.

Oliver Stone's *Wall Street* sequel amounted to a flop. No one understood derivatives, and rather than effectively denounc the post-crash con that was helping to further certify America as an oligarchy, the film glamorized the shrewdness of the con-artists. Just as the lustful violence of the military-entertainment complex incites young viewers to enlist, unadulterated displays of wealth goad the viewer to desire the spoils of greed. Ultimately, Americans received Gordon Gekko as an aspirational character instead of a cautionary tale. In real life, the unmasked villains of American finance would get away with everything. There it was again: a supposed cinematic takedown received as raw aspirational glamour. Could the violence of vast wealth and power ever be understood as objectionable to an American audience? Six years after I sat alone in the theater in Bangkok, my freedom country would elect a dime-store Gekko as president.

What would Mr. Jojo tell his parents? I felt strangely attached to him; despite our limited ability to communicate verbally, I'd become fluent in the way he rolled his eyes at his friends and shook his head laughing while his students tried to impress him with their improvised instrumentation at recess.

From Siam Paragon, I boarded a bus further south to meet my friends in Phuket for the night; in the morning we'd ferry to the islands. The ride to Phuket was fourteen hours. Thai pop was blasting the whole way and the AC was set to "refrigerator." I arrived at the island past the point of hunger and fatigue. It all melted away when I exited the bus into the wet night air. I had to figure out how to get to the hotel where my friends were staying. A fleet of motorbike drivers stood waiting by the bus, and one driver stood waiting persistently while I called my friend. I met his gaze with a flat expression and was surprised that he returned it with a kind eagerness. "Where to?" he asked.

I told him the name of the hotel, and he took my backpack and placed it on the front basket of his bike. I got on the back and he asked, "You okay?"

"Yeah, di ka," I said laughing. *Good.* He started the engine. I clutched the metal bar around the back of the seat as we flew through the night. I clocked the rate at which we sliced the air. It was alarming and dangerous and exactly what I needed.

Soon it started raining, and we reached the bottom of a large steep hill. The ascent began on the wet roads and I gripped the back of the seat. But we were climbing and there was nothing I could do to stop it. On the other side of the hill, the roads were slicker still. I wondered what would happen if we were to wipe out on the road—if the tire caught too steep of an angle and sent us flying. We stopped on the side of the road.

"Sorry," he said, and pulled out two plastic rain jackets from his bag. He gave me the blue, put on the pink, then handed me a helmet from the front basket. I caught his rain-streaked face and high cheekbones in the glow of the street light. Maybe it was because I'd just traversed a country alone, but the intimacy of the gesture seemed meaningful, like we were on an epic adventure together.

It rained harder as we rolled down the hill and continued pouring as we got closer to our destination. The rain rushed two-to-three inches deep over the road; as the motorcycle cut through the water, small waves rippled out toward the curb. We were lost, and he called the hotel while I stood under a bus stop shelter. He called me over to talk to the hotel's front desk, with a familiar gesture that made it feel we knew each other well. We eventually reached the hotel, and I fumbled for my money to pay him. He asked how long I'd be staying, and I almost wanted to invite him to join my friends and me for a late dinner that night. Maybe I was starved for companionship after six months of communicating mostly by reading faces, or maybe I always feel too close to kind strangers. I paid him and wished him a good ride back, and he smiled and said "see you" before jumping on his bike.

On the islands, my friends and I danced to American pop music every night, drank whiskey and Coke out of plastic bags with straws and shared stories of our teaching posts all around the country. I told them about Mr. Jojo, and they were impressed that I made out with a Thai guy as they would routinely avoid eye contact with us. We danced on the beach and in Cowboy-and-Indian theme bars, with Norwegian fire dancers and Thais and

Italians while "Party in the USA" played and Germans sang to "Empire State of Mind."

After our beach vacation, we all traveled back to Bangkok for our exit orientation, to the same hotel where we'd tried to learn basic Thai six months before. In the air-conditioned conference room, an American diplomat with the US Embassy in Bangkok came to thank us for our work and urged us to join the Foreign Service. He had two capital letters for a name and a thick neck. He'd lived in Germany, Iraq and Kuwait and was now serving in Bangkok. As he talked about our service to the government, I suddenly realized that I had in fact been an employee of the US State Department. Our six-hundred-dollar end-of-semester stipend hadn't come from Thailand's purse but America's. I hadn't actually been recruited by Thailand's government to aid in their aspiration toward English as an official second language. I had been an unwitting emissary of my own government, part of its vague mission to "spread democracy."

Thailand borders Malaysia to the south, and Thailand's southernmost three provinces had been engaged in a struggle for liberation led by ethnic separatists for decades, with escalating violence in the previous ten years. Some assigned responsibility for the insurgency to foreign Islamist groups. Just as during the Cold War, Thailand remained a pivotal ideologic and geographic junction between the U.S. and its rotating enemy of the decade. I was a reluctant envoy to begin with, and in the end an explicit diplomatic emissary of the flag I was so hesitant to wave. Realizing all of this just I was about to board a plane home, I felt duped, fooled and ultimately like a complete moron. How could I have not *known*? I thought back to P'Duong urging me to teach the kids about America, and how I'd resisted, not knowing that promoting America was in fact my whole job. If I had known, I wouldn't have been able to get on the plane in the first place. But I was as dumb as Charlie Sheen's Chris, blindly enlisting in a war of cultures to give my life meaning, writing letters home that described a colorful backdrop I didn't understand.

Just as anti-war cinema was a contradiction in terms, my stint as an innocent abroad could never be as simple as I thought or have anything to do with me at all. I came here to see what the world felt like, and maybe I *had* tried to own the world, to throw a net around it—or at least define it.

On the last day of school, some of the students asked me when I was coming back to Thailand. I told them it would be soon.

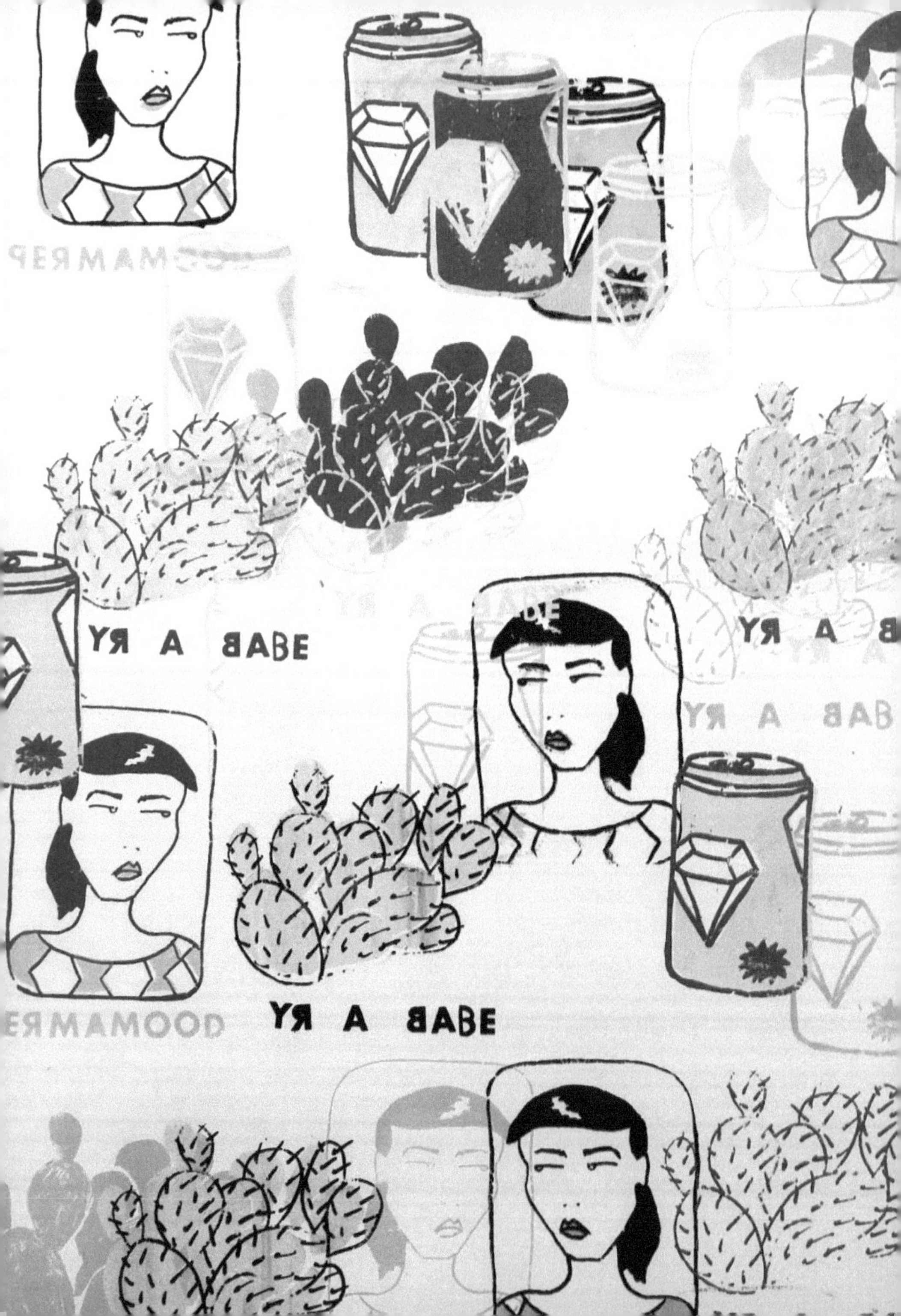

BABE A RY
BABE A RY

Local Legends

I could hear the crickets starting up their buzz from deep within the forest that surrounded us: the low hum of an expectant crowd. I flicked a quick wrist shot toward the goal, and the Figi water bottle hanging by a shoelace on the cross bar responded with a satisfying *thunk*. Another point for Canada. I was rollerblading around an outdoor rink in Michigan, and I was an international roller hockey star.

Only three of us circled the rink, but we made up an entire league. Jake was long and lean with light brown hair parted to the side and the jaw of a runway model. Ben was smaller, with curly hair and bright blue eyes that could affect a deep soulfulness.

Jake was explaining the game to me, and his directions swam shapelessly through my mind.

"So we dump the puck past the opposite net, then all skate behind the red line. We get back in the zone and have to complete three passes before taking a shot on. Everyone has to touch the puck, and we have five shots to score. After that the play's over and the other team's on offense. First team to get to five wins, but they have to win by two."

"Just show me," I said.

I was 25 and back at my parents' place, which had never been my home; they'd moved back to the college town where they'd met. Out of money, I arrived at their door after living on the West Coast and in Thailand. I enrolled in screen printing classes at the art institute in town and began earning $5.15 an hour plus tips as a barista at a coffee shop down the street. To be hired, I was tasked with passing three separate tests to make sure I could differentiate between the five different mochas on the menu and remember how long the spinach and feta turnovers spent on the panini grill. In college I'd only learned how to apply Baudrillardian theory to postmodern texts. I didn't know I should have learned how to apply between twenty and thirty pounds of pressure to the espresso in a portafilter for the perfect shot.

The morning shift at the café started at 5:20, and I'd ride my bike in the dark and start the day pulling timed shots of espresso and downing as many as I could stand before I started to feel sick. Most of our customers were regulars, professors who'd drop their change in the tip jar. It wasn't glamorous, but I'd been bulldozed by the past couple of years trying to pay rent on minimum wage. I needed a break from the unrelenting demands of what turned out to be real life in Great Recession America.

Around this time, the *New York Times* constantly wondered if mine was a generation of basket cases, narcissists or wimps. It noted that "[g]raduates are turning down job offers in high numbers—essentially opting to move back home with their parents if the work offered doesn't match their self-assessed market value," in an article titled "The Why Worry Generation." I found this amusing since all I or anyone I knew did was worry. Perhaps the *New York Times* editors were right, and I deserved the fate of my market value topping out at eight hundred dollars per month. That I was wrong to assume I would be employable doing even the most menial task at some organization with even a vaguely altruistic mission. I'd stuffed envelopes at the Oregon Environmental Council for free. Maybe the wizened editorial boards at the country's finest newspapers had also applied to hundreds of minimum wage jobs when they'd just graduated, with thousands of dollars of student loan debt. Surely there was something I was missing, and this was all my mistake.

Jake and Ben, the other two thirds of the league, were both back home from L.A. after each being left by his girlfriend. They were both from town and had known each other for years. Jake was making salads at a restaurant downtown, and Ben was collecting California unemployment checks from his former life in the film industry.

I first saw Jake while I was steaming milk. He was outfitted in fitted dark Levi's and glasses with vintage frames. He spoke in a soft measured tenor as he ordered double espressos. A tall sophisticated man in a town where everyone else wore sweats over their spray tans? Maybe I could make it work here.

After some small talk at the counter, Jake and I made plans to meet at a local brewery. I learned he was a drummer who was living between his mom's place and a music studio on Lake Michigan. He was working on an album of his own songs while session drumming for indie bands. Despite his perfect skin, he was nine years older than me. Thirty-four was older than a hot person could ever be, but Jake seemed ageless. At the brewery, we got drunk, and kissed. "I'm in love," I texted my sister from the bathroom. "You always are," she answered.

Jake played roller hockey with Ben; they made up national teams and played all the characters; they alone comprised the two teams facing off against each other. I'd played hockey in high school. Our third date was to Hockey Services, a skate shop next to a gun store off the highway. I walked around the store, picking up the blades and spinning the hard plastic wheels. I settled on a pair of slick black Bauers with red wheels and glided around the store. I dug out five twenties from my wallet: The blades were mine, and much more fun than paying my loans.

We headed straight to the outdoor rink. Ben was waiting for us, circling the concrete. I put on my skates and rolled around tentatively on the fresh wheels. I misjudged a turn—the concrete was less forgiving than the ice I was used to. I slipped on a sharp turn, and skidded on my knee. I stood up, wiped the blood, and started practicing my crossovers on the perimeter of the cement oval.

I bought pink laces for my new blades, just as I'd done with my hockey skates a decade earlier as the captain of my high school team. I loved the sport, but I was never a great player. I was good at skating: I loved the feeling of exploding into a sprint down the length of the rink as the breeze ballooned through my jersey, the fine spray of ice that blade carved from the rink at a hard stop. I loved that sound, metal on ice. But I wasn't aggressive or adept at stickhandling. I lacked the size and skill, and most crucially the hunger and drive of a great athlete. By the end of high school, I abandoned it all for my *Rolling Stone* and *Spin* subscriptions and dreams of a freer, cooler future: one that I could construct myself, less ordered by practice times and quantified measures of success. I wanted to escape the dreary confines of life that school and organized sports had primed us for: every moment scheduled, finding meaning in something as ultimately pointless as an athletic contest, a buzzer signaling the abrupt end of our arbitrary endeavor. I would make something all my own.

In our league of three, the "other team" in question was still *us*; we'd just go from embodying our Russian counterparts to the Canadians with offensive possession of the puck while we attempted to score by hitting the Figi bottle hanging in the net. There were eight teams in the league: standard hockey behemoths Russia, Canada and Finland, plus the U.S. and the wild cards Germany, Italy, France and England. Ben, Jake and I all had a player for each team; There were always only three bodies on the rink, but 24 possible personas. Each player had an elaborate backstory. Jake's Russian, Eegore Von, was the most feared player in the league: a hardened ex-con at 18 whom the government had sprung from prison to do his nation proud. My Finn, Jiri, was a beloved veteran who, in a rather Oprah-like fashion, offered giveaways to the (imaginary) crowd by placing bottles of his signature cologne under their seats. Ben's Italian, Ferrari, was a part-time model with a full-time ego. Eddie Vedder, Neil Young and Will Smith were in attendance every time we played at

LA's Staples Center, and Gerry Rafferty would sing the national anthems of both teams.

Along with our players, we also had announcer alter-egos: Jake's Barry provided the majority of the chatter: "I don't know, Jim," he'd say ominously when the Russians struggled to keep up with the Finns late in a pivotal match.

My Jerry was more of an affable color commentator: "The most beautiful sound in the league, folks," when the rubber ball made contact with the Figi bottle, as we imagined it echoing off the boards high up into the crowd.

Jake christened our enterprise, "The Premier World International Fantasy Hockey League," or PWIFHL. We forced our friends to come watch and had a website where we posted player profiles:

> Leading this season's rookie crop is one Jean-Paul Olivier, the young Frenchman with a killer wrist shot and a big mouth. The son of an Olympic curler and a mime, J.P. cut his teeth on the ice in the foothills of the Alps. Earlier this season, J.P. established himself as a presence in the league by trash-talking [Finnish veteran] Jiri in the *International Hockey Tribune*. J.P. is currently vying for a spot on the All-Star team, going up against solid contenders Jamie Murphy and Achek Jones. Should he be snubbed, he can fall back on his film and modeling career, as he's kind of a babe. J.P. also enjoys water skiing, the films of Akira Kurosawa, and ketamine.

Our regular season would be a total of 28 games. Jake kept track of the stats on a piece of lined paper. For an added element of fantasy, the year would be 1984, which Jake had figured had the

same exact calendar as the year in which we were actually existing, 2011. "This year has a magic energy," he said.

"We're basically LARPing," Ben noted one day.

"Emily's experiencing her second childhood," my mom would tell
people. My first had never ended. Physically, I was in the best
shape of my adult life while also drinking lots of Miller Lite. Jake
and I would go out to the rink early, break for lunch at a nearby
sports bar and lace up again until dark. We named the rink "the
Oasis" because it sat, mirage-like, in the middle of a field surrounded by dark green trees. The sun would drop low, the lights
would come on and for a moment, while all my friends were living in the Brooklyn-Portland-Austin matrix, working real jobs
and going out to bars where everyone was hot, it felt like I was
doing something real too, or at least creating a world in which my
teammates and I were stars.

Between games, we'd lazily skate around the Oasis and ruminate on our plans for our actual lives. Ben was moving to New
York. Jake would finally get his big break: a national tour drumming with a well-known band, or selling a song for an ad cam-
paign make to enough money to live for a while. I would eventually figure out how to become an artist, get paid for being me and
spend my evenings on rooftops with well-coiffed and interesting
people.

"Fellini's becoming one of the best players in the league," Ben
said to me about my Italian player one day as we were warming
up. My skating had become seamless: long strides to glide the
length of the rink, quick turns to reverse course. It had begun
to feel like dancing. The hours spent on the rink had made my

thighs newly hard and muscular. My shot was now reliable; my players had as many goals as Jake's and Ben's did.

Some game days we'd roll up to the rink and there would be... other cars. The Doughboys: puffy pale townies missing wheels in their blades who took slap shots while their girlfriends waited in the Tercel with some Jimmy Johns. The Doughboy of the day would toss a glance at our trio and pose the dreaded phrase, "Wanna play a little two on two?"

Gone was the subtle beauty of our contest, of completed passes and setting up a teammate for the perfect snapshot. In two-on-two, I was just a girl again, perpetually subpar, not as fast, a weaker shot, not aggressive enough on defense and unwilling to throw myself underneath a grown man to dig an orange ball out from his stick. But Jake was magic. He could out-skate and out-shoot everyone on the rink while twirling around them as gracefully as a ballerina. Here in the Oasis he wasn't a prep cook living at his mom's. In this game, he won every time.

After a day on the rink, we'd hit dive bars on the far reaches of town and feed the jukebox quarters for Genesis deep cuts. Jake had grown up in these places, with his electrician dad. We'd sit surrounded by the local roughnecks, white guys in their fifties and sixties with prison tattoos and a gruffness to match, a fresh beer and Keno card perpetually within reach. Jake was at home in that world but gazed at it from a comfortable distance through his vintage frames.

While Jake was at the studio on the Lake Michigan coast during the week, we'd talk on the phone for hours. He'd pore over his life decisions, wondering if he should start on another path. "I don't wanna be some old guy playing at local bars. Maybe

I should give it all up... become a bus driver or learn how to make furniture," he'd muse.

I'd murmur "*mmhmm*," trying my best to offer some sort of valuable advice, even though I was just as lost.

What I wanted was something real, anything to hold onto. I wanted a handsome man to make my life real, a temporary fix for everything I was missing. But I barely felt real to myself and could never reveal myself to him. I resented him for meting out barely enough to get by on, and myself for taking it. But I was also keeping him out: attempting to present only my best angles, afraid he wouldn't want the whole story. Somehow, it was comfortable that way: wanting something I could never have, because it didn't exist.

Between games, I drove around town in my mom's car, her Fleetwood Mac CD in the stereo: the soundtrack of my childhood. The melancholy twang of "Gypsy" resonated differently now; it seemed like a song about something that had ended and would never return. The song poured out of the open windows into the yellow afternoon sun. I tried to imagine that this was the life I'd planned all along.

Occasionally Jake and I would approximate a date: drinking dollar beers at the local minor league arena, a farm team for the Red Wings. I wanted to dress up when we went out, put on mascara and a dress, remind Jake I wasn't just a hockey player with a decent snapshot. But our destination was only another hockey game, and I didn't want to appear high maintenance. I never asked him to take me anywhere else.

One night we went to a movie, then back to his place. We headed to the garage so we wouldn't wake his mom and opened some ancient Smirnoff Ices. We grabbed some old hockey sticks and took turns shooting at a mini net. "I don't want this night to be over," he said. He went through the front door of the house and opened his bedroom window so I could climb in. He passed out, and we fell asleep on his printed sheets. In the bright morning light, I crawled back out the window and walked home. I laughed at living a teenage fantasy at 25, somehow sated by feeling as though I'd been chosen by Jake as another cool person in this small town, who matched his commitment to living a creative life.

Some nights, we'd run into his friends from high school at the bar. They were balding dads in their mid-thirties. Jake was watching the Stanley Cup Playoffs with a twenty-five-year-old in jorts and a crop top. At the bar, he'd ruminate on successes of past decades: being in the best local bands, almost making it in LA. I sat and listened, half rapt as his eyes changed from gray to blue to sort of green in the bar's dim light, but wanting to interrupt him to remind him that I was an artist too and that he should ask *me* some questions. I never did. Maybe I wanted too much, something impossible: to be the chic, silent, perfect accessory to the great man, the Bianca Jagger or Anita Pallenberg, and to be the main attraction, the Mick Jagger himself.

At some point, I began to wonder if he might not have the energy to take on the world with me. I was busy imagining my next step back out on my own, to try again to make my way. It was becoming clear to me that he wasn't, and that we were going nowhere, just skating in circles. For a while, I didn't let it bother me too much. I was wide-eyed and twenty-five, with long eyelashes and enough hope and ambition for the both of us.

We passed the summer this way, dancing the length of the rink until it got dark, then eating nachos at a dive bar and making out in his van. One night in August when his mom was out of town, he dropped me off at my house instead of taking me back to his place. I knew it was over.

I texted him passive aggressively late that night: "We don't have to keep doing this if you don't want to."

"That doesn't sound like you," Meredith said when I told her the next day.

Jake called the next day, but I missed it and didn't feel like there was anything more to say.

He avoided my coffee shop for the next eight months.

By the next summer, I'd moved a thousand miles away, to a bigger city where I could get lost and imagine more. I returned to town for a weekend and the PWIFHL commissioners set a date for a game. It felt good to be returning as someone new, someone who had broken out of all those circles I'd skated, thinking they led somewhere. As I stepped into Ben's Jetta for a ride to the Oasis, the distinct scent of his car transported me back to the summer before: hockey equipment sitting in a hot car for months. It was the acrid smell of decay: sweat seeping into the bones of the car itself in the August heat. I was transported to the unquelled longing that had defined that summer, and the strange safety of throwing myself at someone who would never really know me. It was a deep and heavy longing for my life to begin, and a simple longing to be adored.

Since I'd left town, Ben had gotten a place with his girlfriend. They'd planted a garden and weren't going anywhere. Jake had been playing some local shows, and skating.

Ben dropped the orange ball into the concrete rink. "I don't know, Jim..." Jake began.

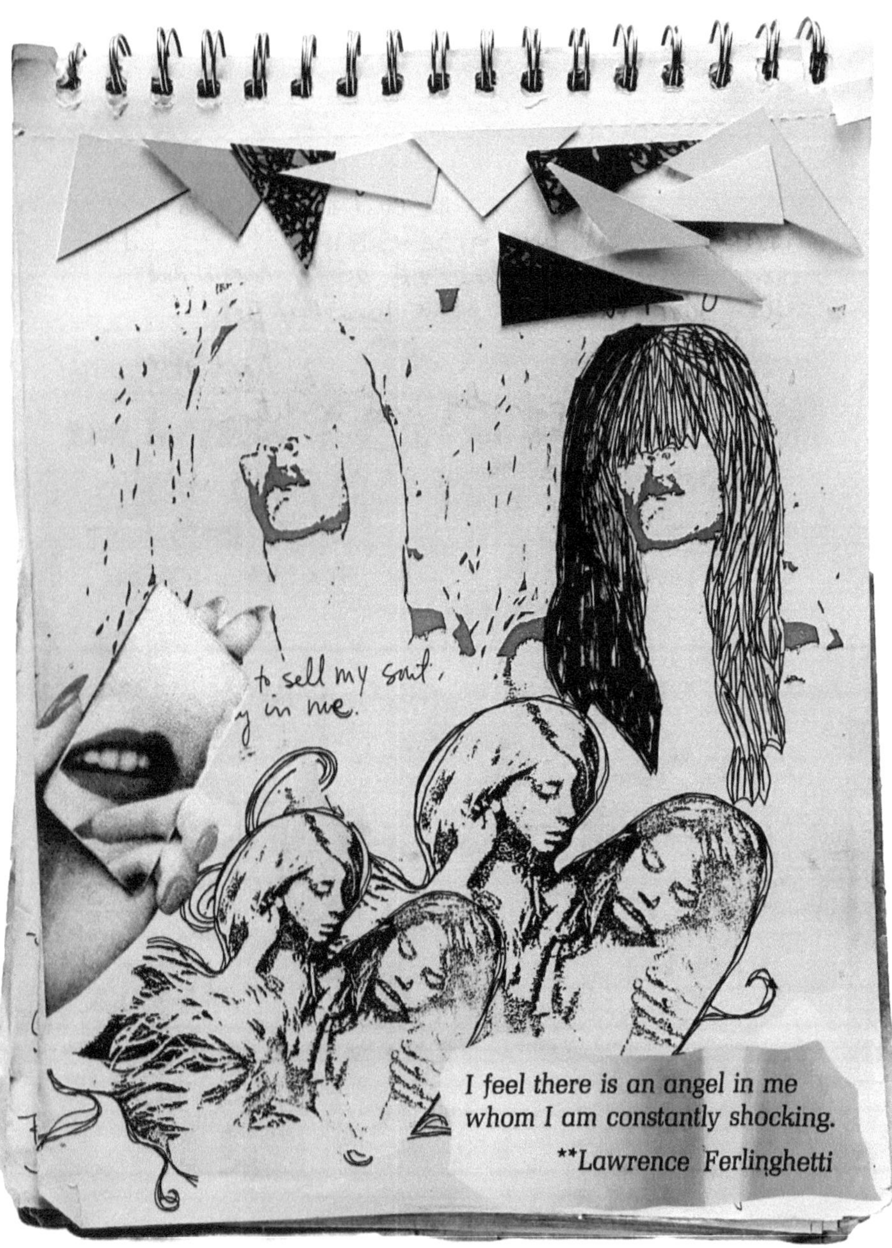
to sell my soul,
in me.
I feel there is an angel in me
whom I am constantly shocking.
**Lawrence Ferlinghetti

Loose Woman

I'm a woman delighted with her disasters. / They give me something to do. / A profession of sorts. I stared over the clouds, and then back at the book on my tray table. Sandra Cisneros' collection of poems, *Loose Woman,* was my companion on the flight. My plane hovered over Los Angeles, which seemed to stretch on forever beneath us, the Earth glittering as dusk deepened to an inky darkness.

I was escaping to LA to see Kelly.

It was the end of a long winter. I was twenty-six and still living in Michigan. My parents had just divorced. I spent most of my free time in the screenprinting studio, and most of my paycheck from the coffee shop on art classes and at the bar with my friends. I reasoned that Andy Warhol probably also took too many tequila shots on weeknights. There was still time for me. Freed from the prospect of a real job or a future to aspire to, my real adolescence had finally arrived. I'd tip-toe into my mom's house two hours after midnight and eat a plate of nachos while watching *Cheers*. Things had recently headed south with Jake, and I was pissed at myself for being so stupid, for allowing myself to be tricked into pouring my attention into a handsome man who wasn't pouring his attention into me.

The year before, Kelly had moved back to the weed farm with her boyfriend, and they were running the operation. They had just broken up, and she was unmoored.

None of this was intentional. Kelly and I were failing to convince ourselves we weren't complete losers, in parallel. Our collective dream of artistic freedom and a paycheck had failed catastrophically, like a bellyflop into a shallow pool. At least we had each other. "Yeah, I feel like my brain was finally like OH SHIT DUH STOP BEING SAD AND TAKE OVER THE WORLD, which of course you're implicated in," Kelly wrote after we talked for hours one day. Our correspondence always buoyed me, reminded who I was and that it was ok to spend my time building little worlds with my art rather than building a resume and saving money for something sensible.

Meanwhile, in the dead of winter, I was busy wandering around my mom's house and trying to entertain myself with my library books and the internet.

10:20 am: Wake up. So. Tired.

11:40: Wake up again. Stumble downstairs with Martin Amis in hand. Put yesterday's coffee in microwave.

12:20 pm: Check email.

12:30: Scan *idealist.org* for jobs.

12:32: Think about updating resume.

12:33: Google image search "bruce springsteen jean vest." Brief scan reveals nothing other than the sad fact that Target sells denim vests. Then a photo of 80s era Bruce in a jean vest over a leather jacket. Not quite what I was hoping for.

12:36: Watch Nelly videos on YouTube.

1:00: Catch up on google reader. Over a thousand unread items! I'm so busy.

1:47: Read item about how some guy from Yale '09 just got a book deal, focusing on the immorality of his generation. Gross.

2:30: Wonder if I can sell the rights to my twitter account to NBC.

2:31: Realize that my twitter account is only retweets of Michael Ian Black and Andrew W.K.

2:32: G-chat to multiple friends about Rihanna's haircut. Send all friends links to Nelly videos.

3:45: Go for a run. Plot strategy to become YouTube sensation via acoustic covers of Nelly and Flo Rida while wearing low-cut shirt.

4:45: Get back, check email. Weekly shower.

5:00: Breakfast.

6:00: Stare at record collection. Momentary indecisiveness over whether to choose Bruce, Hall and Oates or ELO turns to excitement as a I realize I can listen to all of them. Briefly wonder when someone will love me for my record collection rather than for my boobs and ill-tempered personality. Also realize that someone has my Joan Armatrading. And that the riff in Bruce's "Badlands" off of *Darkness on the Edge of Town* is the closest to perfection we may ever confront in this world.

6:17: Stare at collage material. Succeed in making two cards and organizing old magazines chronologically. Thumb through photos from college. Vaguely remember having a reason to live.

8:30: Dinner: popcorn and beer, and bananagrams with Mom. I won, and as usual she accused me of cheating.

9:26: Double check alphabetical order of records. Put on Jackson Browne's "Lawyers in Love," decide again that, while embarrassingly 80s, it's underrated. Draw my own hand.

10:30: "Arrested Development" on Hulu, with almond-milk hot chocolate and kahlua.

11:17: Tobias is blue. LOL.

11:32: Check Facebook to make sure no unflattering photos have been tagged.

11:40: Return to *The Rachel Papers*; another day, another few chapters of Amis.

In Belize, I'd spotted Kelly across the room in the welcome assembly in an outfit that seemed familiar to me, a little striped skirt and stretch poplin tank, something legible in a strange land of constant sun and banana palms. She was tall and busty with dark curls arranged around her face and constellations of freckles swirling around a tiny, pierced upturned nose. She was an environmental studies and English major at Berkeley and also believed that Bob Dylan and Allen Ginsburg had all the answers. But she was completely non-judgmental when the guys in our group expounded on their love of Phish and the cheap knock-off Xanax from the Belizean pharmacy, while I rolled my eyes. She had spent high school learning how to play Led Zeppelin songs on the guitar. She could roll a perfect joint. I was raised on Long Island and the suburbs of Philadelphia, where I saved my babysitting money to spend on platform sandals from dEliA*s.

In Belize, we were in the same Alternative Energies class. We'd pass notes and try to distract our teacher by prodding him about JFK assassination conspiracies when we hadn't done the homework.

"Of course it was the CIA," he'd respond.

Kelly's laugh trilled into a musical shriek if she thought something was really funny. The nicknames we gave each other, Keh and Eh, came from a "Kids in the Hall" sketch. Kelly saw me as I hoped to become: infinite and capable of anything. It's always easier to think more of others than what we think of ourselves: What I questioned in myself, I knew existed in her resolutely. I had infinitely more confidence in her abilities and intelligence than in my own.

Kelly could locate a faith in herself, or the world, or the boys she brought home in a way I never could. She was tenacious and I was tired. I worried that I would be punished for indulging my hedonistic tendencies; Kelly didn't believe in any such retributive balance. The apocalyptic cultural diagnoses of *Adbusters* Magazine wallpapered my psyche while she seemed to take them with a grain of salt. She was rooted in a sense of trust in the ultimate goodness of the world, of fairness and abundance, that I couldn't grasp.

Sending messages across the country to someone I knew would always understand extended back to college, when we'd kept up constant communication. While procrastinating on papers, I'd sit in the library and write her emails.

> From: Emily
> To: Kelly
> I am doing required things (school, work, being an unpaid intern) like 70 hours a week now, which is kind of like what stock brokers do, except without all the money, coke, and affairs.

> From: Kelly
> To: Emily
> i was taking a leak in the bathroom today and written on one of the walls was 'peace (not equal to sign) lack of war' and then in another place it said 'we are all slaves to this corporate plantation'. but then: underneath the latter someone else had written 'your mom's a slave!!' WTF!?

Later, after Kelly left Portland for Colorado and I lingered as long as I could, we traded missives from wherever we were.

> From: Kelly
> To: Emily
> Yesterday I felt like everything happening to me was being perceived by my own brain and thoughts and feelings and location in the space/time calico as totally negative and run-down, like my own goals of self-betterment and -exploration were stupid and small and worthless because there were so many

people in the world who just want to come to a resort ski town for christmas to yell at people "under them" (whatever the hell that means) and throw the weight of their material excess around in an ignorant fashion. But you know what? It forced me to re-evaluate whether or not I'm living an intentional life. Super caffeinated. Bout to go home and strum some Patsy Cline and then watch A Scanner Darkly with a boy who is completely unavailable and that's okay with me now. Thank you for being alive and being my watermark, or maybe a doorway when there's an earthquake.

Now, toward the end of a long Michigan winter, I walked through the gray slush on free afternoons to the downtown public library, in my long blue suede coat with shearling trim while listening to New Order on my iPod. At the library, I found a seat with my stack of oversized art books—Warhol, Bauhaus, Basquiat, Lee Krasner—and sipped from a coffee I wasn't supposed to have in there. Sometimes I'd browse the poetry, looking for an instruction manual to life hiding in the compact volumes.

The copy of *Loose Woman* had a bland brown cover that the library had placed on the paperback for protection, but the lines inside were technicolor. *Oh heartily sorry am I for this right side of the brain/ who has alarmed and maimed and laid me many a day now/ invalid low.* I checked it out and took the tiny volume with me everywhere. Sandra wrote of her partner in a reckless entanglement: *Allow you red wine in bed,/ even with my vintage lace linens. Maybe. Maybe.* Along with disrupting the patriarchal capitalist order, I planned to bridge the wide gulf between who I was and the type of woman who'd draw a tentative line in the sand to her endless succession of lovers: *not on my vintage lace linens. Well… maybe.*

Inspired by Sandra, I scrawled plenty of late-night musings about my purple mouth and black lace underwear and how they respectively would be neither kissed nor seen, not tonight: "Tonight my legs are even smooth, but you won't feel them, you don't feel anything."

What Sandra Cisneros asks of her romantic partner—*I want to know that I knew you/ before I knew you*—I found in Kelly. Now Kelly was adrift in a natural wilderness; I was barely treading water in a cultural one. We needed to place ourselves in the exact opposite situation from where we each currently stood. I called her one night in March while fat snowflakes slowly fell outside the windows of my studio.

"Fuck it, let's just meet up," said Kelly.

"I'm booking a ticket to L.A."

She would drive down, I would fly, and we would drive north up the coast, and figure it out along the way.

After I landed, the California night air alarmingly non-lethal on my thawing skin, we went to a show downtown where guys with Rod Steward haircuts in suits and tight T-shirts sat drinking PBR tallboys.

At the show, Kelly ran into a tall blond friend of her ex. We followed him up into the hills to a white stucco house with people and music spilling into the dark. Kelly vaguely knew the hosts. I looked down at the glittery lights below, the vista a fairy tale I'd been told, a movie I'd seen. The house was sweaty, dark and loud,

and we twirled around the empty living room after pouring ourselves a drink from a makeshift bar with plastic cups and bottles
of booze on the counter. I felt like the ultimate outsider, in town
from my mom's house in Michigan, a million miles from here.

I lost track of Kelly and considered what to do about the
guy who kept trying to dance with me. Instead, I decided to find
Kelly so I wouldn't be stranded here for eternity. "Do you know
where Kelly is?" I asked around the party. Finally, we found each
other. She was wrapped around the tall blond, holding her drink.
"I could climb him like a tree!" she proclaimed. He'd offered us a
place to stay that night. We made it back to his house in Echo
Park; packed cardboard boxes occupied half the living room, and
the kitchen was similarly overflowing with detritus. Kelly and
our host quickly disappeared, and I took my place on the couch
and fell into a deep sleep.

The next morning, I woke up and opened the door to the
bright March sun. The bougainvillea was blooming with such a
deep and bright magenta it seemed to suggest anything was possible. This felt like a place where no one had ever felt the despair
of being twenty-six and tethered to nothing in a never-ending
winter, of silently begging for love and attention from a person
who would never give it to them. I imagined being someone completely different here, someone so grounded and infinite that I
would never even consider looking for some guy who dressed
well to validate my existence. I walked down the street to a café
and sat with Sandra and an iced espresso. *Anarchists who fled/
with my heart thudding on the back/ bumper of a flatbed truck.* I
was ready to be filled with anything that this place and its bright

air had to offer. "This spring will be different," I wrote in my notebook.

Kelly met me at the café after she left the tall blond. We were always falling in single-serving love then. Love to go, love with sugar and cream, disposable love. We drove to Venice. We ambled down the boardwalk, watching the waves, and browsed racks of cheap sunglasses. I bought a pair of knockoff black Ray-Bans with gold embellishments, and Kelly chose pink plastic heart-shaped frames. "I think we each found our auras in sunglasses form," she said. We drove out to Joshua Tree, gleefully dwarfed by those majestic aliens as we walked among the trees. I basked in the deep dry landscape, as deliciously, vitally foreign, as anywhere on the planet. I felt completely new in the weightless air, absolved by the air that holds on to nothing. I imagined being a member of the Eagles, or any carefree, long-haired white man in head-to-toe denim in the 70s, indestructible enough to transcend the material realm through peyote and tequila, immune to any responsibility or concerns about a bank account.

When we were back in L.A. that night, Kelly spent hours on the phone with her ex. I didn't understand why she had to talk to him at all; their time together was over. I paced the sidewalk while she sat on the curb as he tried to relitigate the end of their relationship. I'd never been part of a long-term couple, and couldn't grasp the gray areas between the black and white of love that I believed in.

The next day, we stopped into a coffee shop in Silver Lake. Everyone was sitting around staring at their laptops and wearing fedoras. I told Kelly loudly while we waited in line that I'd recently read that people with trust funds are actually, on average, miserable. Learning that had coincidentally made me less miserable.

"Wow, I think you managed to piss off everyone in there," she said as we walked out. I shrugged.

From L.A., we headed north to the Bay Area. We stopped on the 101 to look out at Big Sur, over the turquoise ocean, the wind whipping our hair into our mouths. I stared out at the ocean, transfixed. It was a deep blue-green that seemed of another planet from the Atlantic that I'd swum in during my summers in New Hampshire and New Jersey growing up. It matched the ring I'd bought in Berkeley years earlier.

That night in Oakland, we stayed up late talking like we had countless nights before. We were staying with Ryan, our sweet bearded friend who'd generously offered us his room while he took the couch.

"L.A. is INSANE," We shrieked that night in his bed.

"The fedoras."

"Christ I know. This is seriously who's writing our media."

"Okay, also what *is* a web series?"

We both looked at each other. "Should we... move there????" We squealed and cackled into the pillows and kicked our feet under the covers, tossing the sheets up.

"Yes!!!! It makes so much sense!!"

"Oh my god. We're gonna have to spend like eight dollars on a PBR and hate it but it would be SO funny."

"That's literally so dumb but honestly we REALLY should. We could make a movie!"

"Oh my god. It's seriously perfect. But we have to make a pact right now that we'll be honest with each other if we're getting too Hollywood."

"...Should we make a web series?"

The next morning, we walked around Berkeley under a warm gray sky, where I marveled at all the little front yard succulent gardens in all their hundred shades of green. There was a salon on our path.

"Should I do this?"

"YES GIRL."

A few hours later, I emerged with bleached hair, charged to my credit card. I felt like a simulacrum of myself that was realer than the real me, or like I had emerged as my own twin. But instead of an evil twin, one that shed all my weaknesses. "You know they say blondes have more fun," Joe the stylist told me. I reapplied a coat of red lipstick. "If I have any more fun, I think I'm gonna die," I told him, pouting in the mirror.

That night, Ryan's Honda wound through the streets of Oakland as Kelly passed the Maker's Mark back to me and turned up The Weeknd. I rolled down the window and stuck my head out, tasting the California air where the tiny soft succulents grew. We were on our way to a club where we would meet up with Ryan and Kelly's friends from college. They were all working toward establishing their careers and vaguely amused by Kelly's and my current state, aimlessly roaming the Pacific Coast like semi-domesticated animals.

"Spirit in the Sky" was playing and I could feel the bass emanating up through the ground to my feet like something primal and eternal, so I didn't feel like talking about the Meaning Of Obama or the recession or the cutthroat rental market in Oakland. "That's where I'm gonna go when I die, gonna go up to the spirit in the sky:" I twirled and stomped away from the group to that ancient rock-and-roll song about god and death. "Never been a sinner, never sinned."

"You have a nice ass," Kelly and Ryan's handsome friend said later that night.

"Well, that's true but my ass is the least interesting thing about me."

"Okay... you have a penchant for chaos."

"Okay, that's better."

"Wanna get a cab?"

They say I'm a beast./ And feast on it. When all along/ I thought that's what a woman was.

Kelly and I left Oakland after brunch the next morning and headed to Portland. There, we slept in Lilly's living room and Kelly fell in love again, a couple of times. We stayed up late, snorted lines off a table with our friend as she told us she was going back to school to become an autism specialist. Her boyfriend put another record on the turntable. Through the window, the moon shone bright white. Michigan seemed so small and far away, as if it was nonexistent. I was adrift, attached only to this room and the people in it. I felt my awareness of the moment, in a living room with cornflower blue walls and windows with white trim and white linen curtains hovering above my skin and entering my body, coursing through me, and felt that anything could happen, that I existed in the world and could bend it to my will. *I'm for emotions running amok tonight,/ breaking china and getting fucked.*

In the morning, Kelly drove me to the airport. We hugged for a long time, crying in each other's hair. That night, I sat in the Portland airport with a paper cup of green tea, Sandra and a tiny flicker of courage. "I'm blonde, drafting poems on my cell phone and moving to L.A. Fuck you," I wrote in my journal to every guy who never even tried to bring red wine into my vintage lace linens. But it was mostly to myself, for ever being afraid. *I'm loony as a June bride./ Cold as a bruja's tit./ A pathetic bitch. / In short, an ordinary woman,* said Sandra.

"Same," I thought.

We never moved to L.A. Kelly headed back to Portland the next month, and I moved to Boston. In my first, broke season there, I made a rare non-essential purchase of *Loose Woman*; I special-ordered it from the local bookstore and spent thirteen dollars that I needed for groceries. But I needed more to own it, to be guided by it.

I brought the book with me when I moved to Austin. The night was warm, and late under the glow of porch lights and the hum of crickets in the yard. I sat drinking mezcal on ice and leafing through Cisneros's collection. The lines I underlined tell their own story: *I am evil. Without guilt. Primordial exquisiteness. Arrogant as Manifest Destiny. The Aztec love of war in me. Emotional anarchist. The elegance/ of your jaguar mouth.* Years after I first read Sandra on our trip, some lines still resonate, some just as faint echoes.

"Time frightens... it is made of qualitative jumps, irreversible choices, occasions which will never return:" a Guy Debord quote I copied into my journal when I lived in Portland. At 23, I lived in terror of losing time, of my youth and life being consumed by concerns of labor and capital, of not spending it being in love. Terror of losing the infinitesimal flicker of art to a bloodthirsty nation I constantly owed money to. Terror of the desire for freedom becoming only a memory, and then letting even that slip away.

In my mid-thirties I let time escape like water through my fingers. There's nothing else to do. Art and freedom appear in flashes when not swallowed up by work, making transfers between savings and checking, the mechanisms of keeping oneself alive.

Some people will read a loose woman as a sorry slut, a kind of joshua tree who indulges her untrammeled desires and will deservedly pay for that indulgence with eternal loneliness, cast out of the kingdom of the lovable. I realize now that the looseness of this woman is in her porousness, allowing the world to filter through her. She never emerges unscathed but is all the richer for it. *Still hopeless. Still writing poems/ for pretty men. Half of me alive/ again.* Sandra and her sharp-eyed coven of loose women might not keep the man, but they keep the poem. Which is infinitely more valuable.

Digging through a long-lost folder buried in my archives, I came across an email Kelly wrote to me when she had left Portland, and I was still there:

i just read your letters finally, your beautiful nostalgic poem,
and felt a little light beautiful sadness in my heart, and realized that while we go scribbling away our thoughts and poems
and reeling half-phrase of pain, sadness, heartbreak, nostalgia,
overwhelming beauty... we are only attempting to articulate
what this fucked up feeling is, of being 23 and having no
answers. everything is worth talking about and everything is
worth penning on a torn magazine page and sending to someone you love, and that's why i love you. i hope you never stop
writing me things because they are beautiful.

We still send letters back and forth, and I send them imagining her holding a tin can to her ear, connected to my own by a
thousand-mile string, and I know she will always know exactly
what I mean. "You've never made a wrong decision in your life,"
she says as I'm wavering on some routine life drama. It doesn't
matter what the truth is; I will believe her.

Kelly came to visit me in Austin from Missoula where she
teaches writing at the university, sells her ceramics, and lives
with her boyfriend. We drank espresso, got pedicures, traded
essays we were working on, and fell asleep giggling together. On
Saturday night, we met up with my boyfriend and played pool.
As the night ended, we negotiated a means of getting her back
to my place so I could go home with him. I worried about being
a bad friend and a bad host. Kelly brushed off my mild protests.
Kelly gestured to him while he was at the bar. "Who knows how
long this guy's gonna be around; you're stuck with me for life."

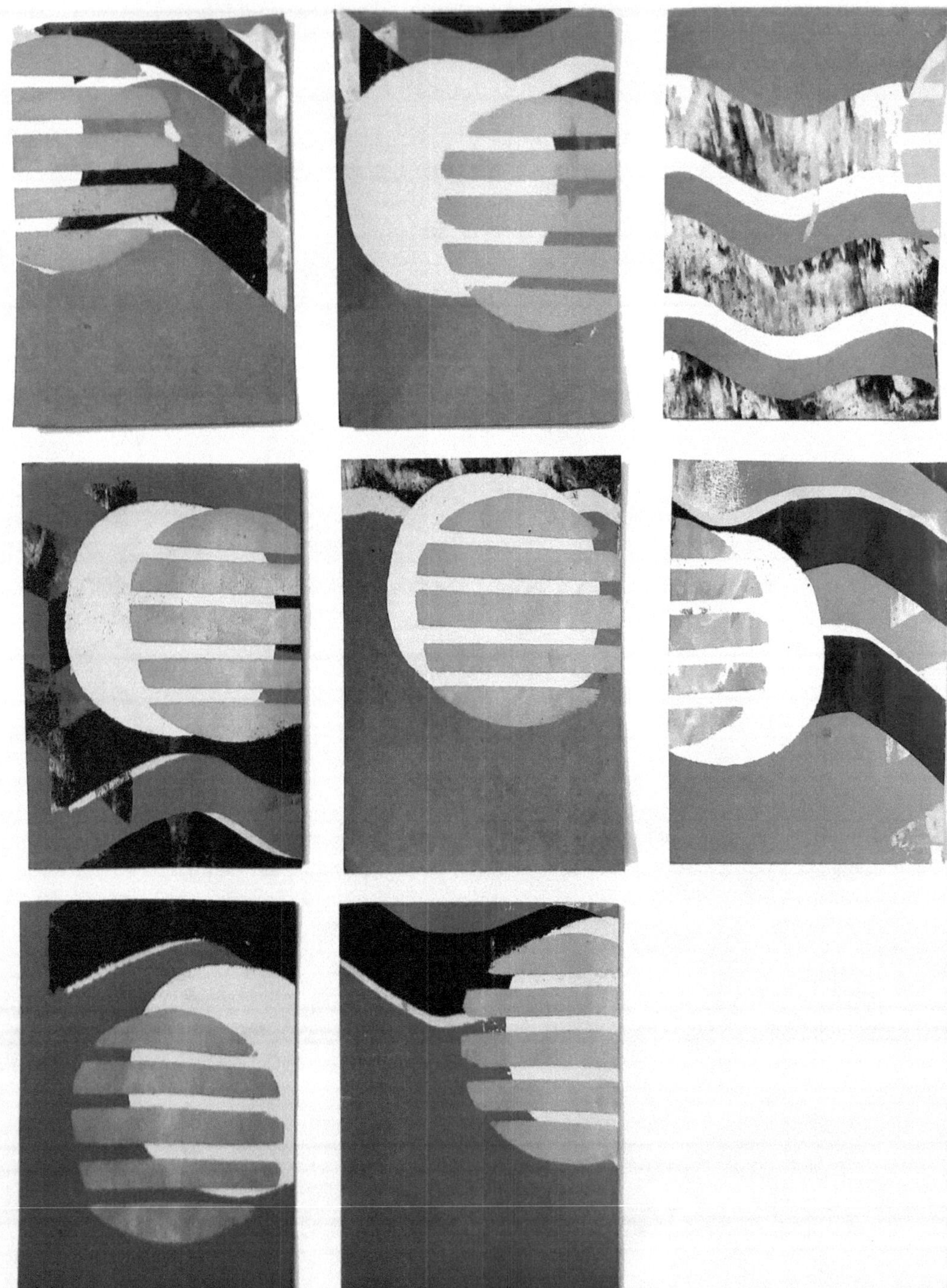

The Empire Builder

I grabbed underwear out of my luggage and stuffed them into my backpack between my journal and my toothbrush. I walked up a few steps to coach seating. The Empire Builder was scheduled to leave at four o'clock from Seattle. In preparation for the ride, I bought a box of Annie's granola bars, which joined a handful of mini bottles of Tennessee bourbon in the bottom of my bag. I'd been visiting Meredith, who gave me a bag of fresh Washington cherries when she dropped me off at the train station. That morning, we'd seen an exhibit of Mick Rock's photography in Seattle's Museum of Pop Culture, featuring enlarged black-and-white prints of David Bowie, Iggy Pop and Lou Reed in their youth. One image showed David Bowie reclining, eyes closed, in a train's sleeper car; the caption noted that he was terrified of flying and preferred to cross the U.S. by rail. I remembered reading somewhere that during his "Young Americans" era, Bowie subsisted on only cocaine, peppers and milk. I found an empty pair of seats and looked out, my forehead pressed against the cool window, as the summer sun hung low over a deep blue sky.

I had recently completed a writing residency in rural Washington. I opted for something different on the way home instead of another cross-country flight. I imagined the tidy confinement of a sleeper car, a cozy compartment of my own from which to wistfully stare out the window. When booking tickets, I learned that a sleeper car of one's own for the 2,206 mile ride from Seattle to Chicago cost nearly a dollar per mile—affordable only to the Aladdin Sanes among us. I settled for a seat in coach at a cool $180. Certainly less cinematic, but I'd still have a window and the same endless expanse of track to peer out from. The landscape began slowly rolling by as the train pulled away from the station. In 45 hours, I would arrive in Chicago on July 4th.

I was thirty-one, responsible only to my after-school teaching job in Boston. I subbed at the school for extra money, and in the summers emptied my savings account to travel or come to residencies like the one I'd just finished. My most valuable asset was a bike. A fourth grader I worked with—who'd pressed the back of her hand to my forehead when she worried I was sick—asked me about school shootings and told me she was afraid to go to high school. I attended protests on Sundays and made micro-donations to the ACLU and ignored the nagging sense of the futility of it all. My long relationship with someone I loved constantly teetered on its edge before righting itself, only to teeter again. The New England winters never really seemed to end, only to break for a quick recess.

I was getting older and the sea levels were rising, two catastrophic processes that showed no signs of abating. Time seemed to be running out: for a habitable world and in my own life for becoming what was meant to be. I was waiting for something to happen: a flash of inspiration or courage that would change my life. In lieu of all that, just to shake myself loose from the usual, I put myself on a train across America.

The Empire Builder embarked on its inaugural journey in 1929, running from Portland or Seattle to Chicago. Every year, it delivers thousands of passengers back home or carries them away to some other far-off destination. In the summer months, the train employs Park Service rangers to narrate the sights from the observation car; they act a bit like baseball announcers. They offer a play-by-play of the natural and cultural history of the landscape. Passengers watching through panoramic windows that curve up to the roof ask them questions about birds.

Bill and John were both around sixty, dressed in starched khaki uniforms and simultaneously exuding a staid professionalism and a giddiness that *this* was their job. Bill was mustachioed and solidly built, John was trim with a British accent. As the train curled alongside the Puget Sound away from Seattle, Bill noted that we might catch a sighting of a cormorant, seal or orca out the train window. Hopeful, I scanned the water for movement. I didn't see any charismatic marine mammals but knowing they might be lurking beneath the surface of the water was thrilling enough.

Further east in Sultan was the site of "Woodstock before Woodstock," the 1968 Sky River Rock Festival, which featured the Grateful Dead and Santana. We continued to Wallace Falls ("higher than Niagara Falls," said Bill), and on to Index, Washington, site of a gold boom in the 1880s. We raced into the new Cascade Tunnel ("the longest tunnel in the lower 48!" chirped John). The rangers made a brief reference to the Chinese workers who had built the rail and blew out the mountain to make way for the tunnel we were riding through. Later, reading up on the train line, I learned that the Chinese laborers were treated as expendable, subhuman, as they worked to build the rail that would render the continent traversable for the first time. I'd become familiar with the process of reorienting myself to far darker truths than the ones I'd been taught as a child.

Three weeks earlier, I'd stared out the window over my residency desk, taking in the cold late spring of the Washington mountains. The residency was housed in an empty elementary school that had been abandoned decades ago after the local mines went bust and the town's population plummeted. I had a chilly eight-hundred-square-foot classroom to myself to sleep and write in: not far off from the writer's garret I'd dreamed of as a kid. Next to the main building, an abandoned courtyard with a faded mural of Pacific Northwest flora and fauna led to an empty echoing gym. Between writing sessions, I ran laps in the gym, which smelled of fresh varnish, as if it had been recently resurfaced for a basketball team that would never return. I marveled at and delighted in the desolation, hoping that this place, completely detached from any reality I'd ever known, would draw something indelible from me.

Each day as the morning fog burned off, hummingbirds fluttered in the huge pink blossoms outside my window, treading the air with a sheer will I couldn't begin to relate to. Logging trucks rolled by my window at regular intervals. On my second day in town, while mailing some postcards, I was bitten by a gray Airedale terrier named Shadow. He charged me while his owner called "Shadow! Shadow!" and then he sunk his teeth through my jeans and into my calf. My shock was mitigated by the rueful acknowledgement that I couldn't last long in Trump country without being attacked. The bite was shallow: I recovered quickly.

Mostly, I was glad to feel fully removed from my usual routines, the well-tread paths between work, the grocery store, the coffee shop and the bar, the alarms set and the snooze buttons hit. The air itself felt wider here. Alpine goldenrod burst from the damp green expanse of earth, dotting the endless wild landscape like dappled sunlight. In the evenings, the sky over the Cascades seemed to ignite, streaked with wisps of neon orange and pink. On a few nights during our stay, our daily word count goals nearly reached, the other writers and I ambled down the hill to the Headquarters Bar for a beer, where our faces were unfamiliar among the other patrons in this town of 200. Shadow barked frantically from a truck in the parking lot. We joined in on karaoke, and fended off advances from the local guys at the bar, who didn't know men can't approach strange women in public any more.

I envisioned my train ride home as an extension of the residency: Riding the Empire Builder, I hoped to access some truth that remained unknowable in a mode of stasis. In my seat, I thought again of David Bowie's young free image suspended in the amber of black-and-white photos, unencumbered by the particular darkness of this moment. I wondered if listening to only David Bowie for the remainder of the summer would successfully transport me even partway out of the current era and solve at least some of my problems. I could attempt to crawl out from under the crushing weight of this extended period by living vicariously through his freedom and freakiness. Maybe he would shift my mood and reveal some truth, teach me something eternal that I was too blocked, too scared, too earthbound to realize on my own. That night, as darkness fell outside the train, I settled further into my seat, poured a whiskey nip into a can of seltzer and cued up a David Bowie album on my iPod. We were heading east, away from the setting sun and into the lavender night. The first few chords of "Rebel Rebel" rang in my ears like a language I'd learned a long time ago, somewhere far from here. *"Hot tramp, I love you so."* I looked out the window as the dark trees rushed past underneath the stars.

The next morning, I awoke to the sounds of John and Bill's broadcast from the observation car. I laid across the two plush seats with a travel blanket and pillow, which served as a sufficient bed. I lifted my eye mask and checked my phone. It was seven. White summer sunlight poured in through the wide windows. I sat up and stretched myself awake; we were in western Montana. I walked through a few cars to the back of the train and bought a watery coffee from the snack bar. A short staircase led me to the observation car on the train's second floor: Here I could absorb John and Bill's geography lesson in person. The observation car was laid out like a diner, with fiberglass tables and vinyl booth seats. I slid into a booth and looked around. Most of my fellow travelers up here were a bit older than me, enjoying the trip with friends or their partners. They looked clean and less rumpled than I felt after 6 hours of sleep across two seats. John and Bill were relaying an amusing anecdote about a cargo truck losing all its corn and bears happily discovering the spoils months later. The corn had fermented in the interim, conjuring a satisfying image of a group of intoxicated black bears. *"Drunk bears,"* I scribbled into my notebook.

The train skated along the southern edge of Glacier National Park. Mountains loomed outside the north-facing windows. "Make sure you take a look at those glaciers," said Bill. "They won't be here in ten or fifteen years." I looked for them; squinting and finding nothing, I wondered if they were already gone. *"Bear grass, lily family. Continental divide. Wild horses,"* I wrote, trying to keep up with the rangers' narration. I kept my eye on the horizon, searching for those horses.

Outside the large windows, the sky was endless and blue. For ten years I'd been steeling myself against the moment when life becomes more about remembering to buy dish soap than noticing the steady rate at which the clouds move across the sky on a bright summer day. Lately, the days seemed to rush by faster than I could account for them. I would get older, and the ice caps in Glacier National Park would disappear. The earth and I were both expiring by the moment. I thought about how the train was built in the twenties when the country's era of cultural expansion and establishment as a global empire was still ahead of it, a distant glowing dream. Now the country and its future seemed to be crumpling as quickly as a leaf in a fire. The empire was being hollowed out and sold for parts. A man at a nearby table in a cowboy hat from Grand Rapids, Michigan, talked to another passenger about his career selling corporate office furniture. Whom does life in America actually work for, I wondered. My attention drifted skyward again. "I had so many dreams," cooed Bowie, "I made so many breakthroughs."

East of Glacier lies Blackfeet Nation. A group of middle-aged women with highlighted bangs joined my table as I looked out at the reservation. I worried they might ask me if I knew Jesus, so I busied myself with my journal. Larger than Delaware, the reservation is a vast expanse of land with a population density of three people per square mile. Further on, piles of discarded mattresses, tires and washing machines formed small mountains, like an art installation implying the general mistake of humanity's existence on the planet.

The next day was the fourth of July. I looked out at this expanse—an unmistakable totem of a people successfully colonized, brutalized, and all but exterminated by the US government. A woman at my table remarked: "It doesn't look very nice."

The reservation disappeared behind us, and we forged ever onward through the empire.

Bill and John departed the train once we reached the middle of Montana. I soon realized why: there's nothing but the mostly flat expanse of the upper Midwest for the remainder of the ride.

I left the observation car and walked back downstairs to my seat in coach. "How far are you going?" asked the girl on the other side of the aisle. I told her I was flying home to Boston after the line ended in Chicago. "Take me with you!" she pleaded. Her name was Cassie, and she'd been visiting her brother in Seattle as a trial run to see if she should move there. She worried it was too expensive and was headed back home to Minot, North Dakota. She'd taken courses at a for-profit college and was on the hook for thousands in debt. She really wanted to be a baker, she told me. "I just want my life to mean something," she said.

My neighbors were all younger than me and traveling by rail for the utility of cheap travel, not in a misguided bid for some epiphanic journey. Two sisters from Washington, wrapped up in tightly in blankets and neck pillows, were taking the train all the way to New York to see Times Square and camp out on Broadway for cheap tickets. The younger sister made sandwiches from bread and peanut butter they'd packed as the older sister touched up anime drawings on her iPad.

A hiker on the Pacific Coast Trail abandoned the route because he'd run out of money and spent the last of it on a ticket home to Minnesota. He planned to do some more construction work until he made enough to return to the trail. "I can't wait to get back," he said with a far-off look in his eyes.

Cody, in his early twenties, was working a low-level tech job in Seattle, couldn't afford the company housing and was going home to his parents' in Southern Illinois. "It sounds dumb," he said. "But I've been reading *The Secret* and I really believe that you manifest your reality. I know this is not a setback."

"Why didn't you fly the whole way if you could afford it?" one of the sisters asked me.

"I don't know," I shrugged. "I just... thought it would be fun."

She turned back to her iPad.

A few hours later, as an orange sun snuck below the top of the windows, we stopped in Minot. "Good luck!" I called to Cassie as she pulled her suitcase off the rack. She turned around and waved. Later, the pink sky was softly reflected in the wet fields of North Dakota. It was a landscape of quiet beauty, still light at 9:30: the land itself blushing. *What gorgeous country*, I wrote in my notebook, *that I would be afraid to set foot in*. The conservative politics, the oil boom that begat a violent crime boom, makeshift towns populated exclusively by lonely men. An empty stretch of land punctured by oil rigs, the extracted resource the only point of value for American earth. The election the year before seemed to be the final blow to a country with a million little fractures. We seemed less willing to admit that those cracks had always been there. As a kid, I spent my summers on a New Hampshire beach. Every Fourth, we'd watch the Americans defeat the British in Revolutionary War reenactments, an enduring, simple fairy tale that we loved to watch because we were the good guys. The beauty of the summer sky mirrored in the fields, both ordinary and breathtaking, called to mind Alice Walker's remark, "I love this land. I'm not crazy about the nation."

I awoke early again the next morning. It was July Fourth. The sky was the light gray of a windless and humid summer day. We were in Minnesota now, winding through small towns, rushing across the Mississippi. Outside my window, Independence Day 5k racers bounced along in American flag capes. Through Wisconsin, the landscape remained wide with the electric summer green of grass and trees until the terrain slowly became denser with houses as Chicago grew closer.

That night in the airport, I charged a twelve-dollar beer to my credit card while waiting to board my final leg home; I wouldn't get the bill for a while. I flipped through the notes I'd taken on the train ride; I hadn't come up with much more than a few scribbled lines about the plants and animals along the route. Nothing had been revealed to me about America other than that it was too vast in its violence and beauty to imagine, even while staring at it. I watched through the airport window as fireworks soared over the city, in the middle of a country that now seemed bigger and more unknown to me than ever. "We live for just these twenty years/ do we have to die for the fifty more?" crooned David Bowie as the sky above the city lit up with its fire show.

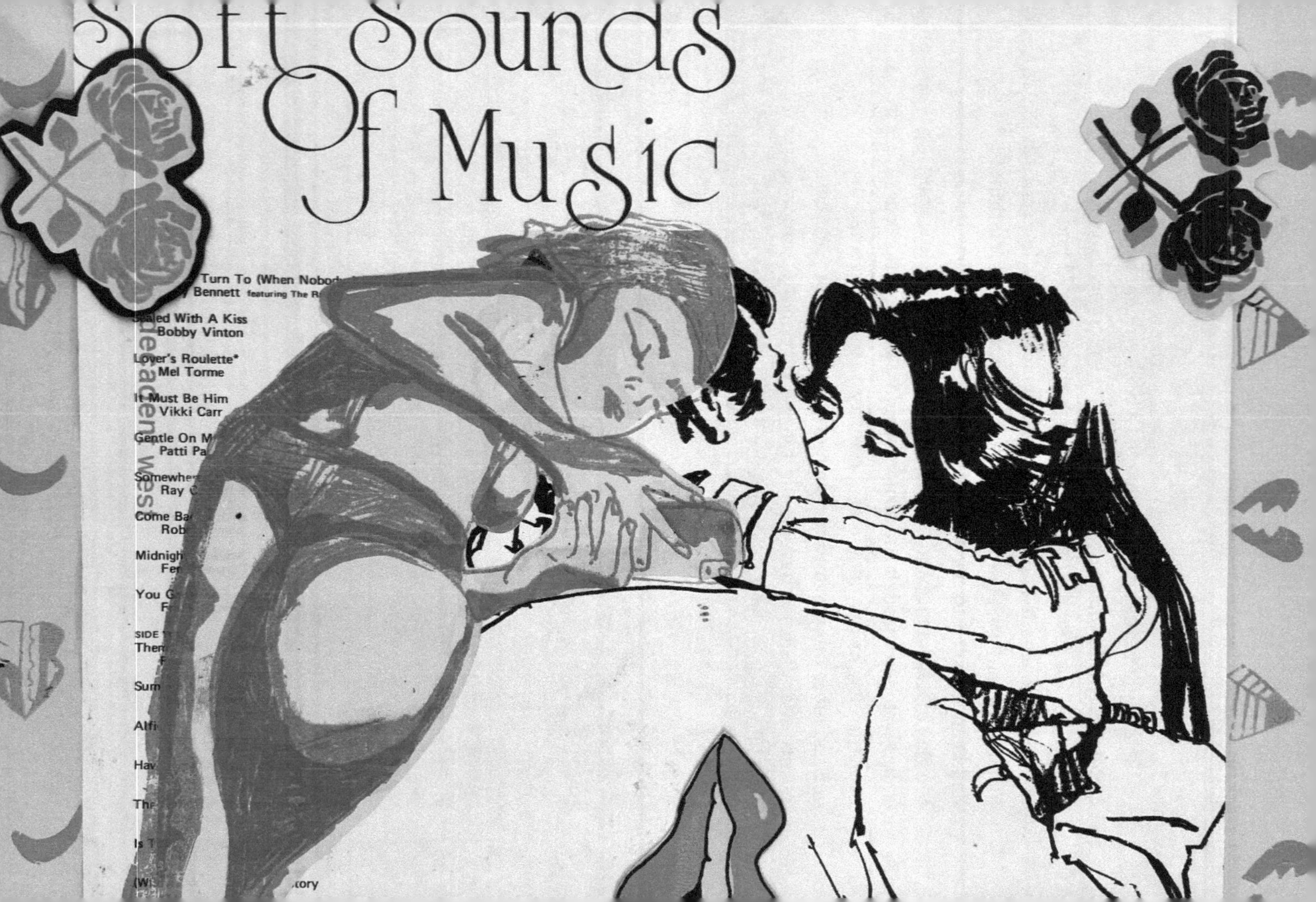
Soft Sounds Of Music
Turn To (When Nobody
Bennett featuring The R...
Sealed With A Kiss
Bobby Vinton
Lover's Roulette*
Mel Torme
It Must Be Him
Vikki Carr
Gentle On M...
Patti Pa...
Somewher...
Ray C...
Come Ba...
Rob...
Midnigh...
Fer...
You G...
Fr...
SIDE T...
Ther...
F...
Sum...
Alfi...
Hav...
Thr...
Is T...
(Wi...

Are you there Richard Linklater? It's me, Emily

I like movies with no plot. Obsession with plot strikes me as vaguely biblical: fake and simplistic. Taken to its logical conclusion, plot is a bunch of adults on steroids in superhero costumes saving the world.

Slacker has no plot. I watched it in my mid-twenties. The film's characters are people I'd met over and over: young people who weren't on a path toward a career and didn't want to be, who sought first to exist in the moment. We rode our bikes to neighborhood shows and stayed up too late talking or following each other into messy bedrooms. There were no clocks tracking a schedule we had to hew to, no dollars in savings accounts, no constant stream of ambient information all the time. There was less data, fewer metrics, no notifications buzzing endlessly from our phones. Our current technolords were in their infancy then, when everyone bought their lines about "bringing the world together." Watching *Slacker*, I recognized something close to the ecosystem that comprised my own reality.

Linklater's camera follows a host of characters making their way through Austin, ambling unhurriedly though town and their day, ready to be distracted by whoever they run into. Theirs are not set schedules, and their lives are seemingly without agenda. None of the characters seem interested in fame, status or money. They wander while considering caste systems and puncturing the reality of mass culture. "Do you ever want to get the hell out of this country?" one woman asks her companion. Is suffering inherently negative? Is working to alleviate it by helping others a distraction from working on oneself?

While I was completely engrossed in *Slacker* and found myself in conversation with the characters that drift through 90s Austin, a spiky thought occurred to me: Is this movie making fun of us? A guy tells a girl he ran into: "Still unemployed.... Still in this band; we've changed our name. We're the Ultimate Losers now."

Conversation turns to Smurf colonies and Brian Eno's *Oblique Strategies*, relationships that threaten to shrink you, moving on from rejection. Were human beings made to be happy and free? If so, why are we always trying to confine ourselves to systems that strip us of happiness and freedom? The viewer never spends much time with a single character as the camera is constantly moving, wandering on to the next. I could relate. Was the freedom and possibility of that time owing to the fact that it was a different era in history, or was it because I was twenty-four?

Rewatching *Slacker*, it's hard not to wonder if Richard Linklater is looking at 20-somethings who sit around in cheap bars, talking about their lives and the world, about politics and their relationships, with their friends and roommates and strangers, and deeming it all a waste of time. The film is called *Slacker*. Is the film's thesis that we were aimless, rootless, wasting our time and our potential? Were we all ultimate losers?

But Linklater is on his characters' side: "Slackers might look like the left-behinds of society," he said in a 1991 *Austin Chronicle* interview with himself. "But they are actually one step ahead, rejecting most of society and the social hierarchy before it rejects them."

He notes that slackers are viewed as people who skip out on the realities of life. But what if they're attempting to redefine those realities, or at least make their own? A more modern view of slackers, Linklater noted, is of people "who are ultimately being responsible to themselves and not wasting their time in a realm of activity that has nothing to do with who they are or what they might be striving for."

During the great recession that began in 2008 and stretched on for years afterward, older generations decided that the children of those hardworking model Americans, the baby boomers, were lazy, ego-driven, sext-crazed narcissists.

"We're aware of the past, informed, cynical in a healthy way, and have a great sense of irony," said Linklater of his generation. "Who could spend such formative years in the 1970s and 1980s and not have that ironic edge?" His coming-of-age era and resulting characteristics could also be applied to post-9/11 and Bush-Era America.

I made ten dollars an hour then, and whatever did not go to rent and the water bill was spent on two-dollar drafts and brunch. But the people I'd met since I finished college who were under- or unemployed weren't unmotivated; despite the dire circumstances of the early 2010s, everyone I knew was searching for a way to reimagine the world, to dream into existence an alternative, a better way to spend their lives. With our low-paying jobs and disinterest in traditional careers, we might have looked like slackers, but we were trying to carve out a new space that left room for living: even if that was just walking around together, talking and thinking, while looking at the world. What some called slacking was, to me, paying life the respect it deserved: to live in each moment, to prioritize experience over collecting expensive clothes and new furniture, to move slowly and intentionally, observing the world and trying to metabolize what you saw.

The summer I was 27, I was living in Boston and working in the shipping and receiving department of the Harvard Book Store. The pay was the minimum wage of $7.25 plus an extra fifty cents per hour to cover the wear and tear on my body from lifting all those boxes full of books. It felt strange to put a price on the slow deterioration of my bones and muscles, especially such a low one. But receiving the books and entering them into the system meant that my coworkers and I had first claim to the damaged books. My weekly pay was two-hundred and eighty-seven dollars. I applied for food stamps but couldn't take the call from the bookstore basement on the clock so I never got them. It was summer, so I could ride my bike five miles each way without worrying about snow and ice and didn't have to spend four dollars a day on the T: There was no way I could afford it. I worked at a cafe on Sundays so I could pay my phone bill. I had attempted to slack, to live a life I chose, guided by art and books and ideas instead of capital and possessions. Instead, I was working constantly and never had enough money.

At the time, I was living in a first-floor apartment in Boston with my sister and our roommate. The apartment cost $1850 per month, and we each paid $617. It was the most I had ever paid in rent, and the apartment's appliances were older than all of us. The apartment contained thousands of cubic feet of air we couldn't afford to heat.

The apartment was heated with oil. The fuel tank in the dark dusty basement held one hundred gallons, and it cost around $800 to fill, a sum that the three of us never had. Instead, we only bought twenty-five gallons at a time, which cost $250. That would last about two weeks. It cost an extra $25 if the tank needed to be primed because it was completely empty, which it always was by the time we ordered more. When the tank was empty because we had stretched our luck too far, waiting till payday to call the oil company for a delivery, the hum of the heater would abruptly cease, an uneasy silence ringing out, and the temperature would quickly start to drop. The oil was delivered from Dorchester, and they would get to us when they could.

Between the three of us, we didn't have enough furniture to fill the large rooms, or rugs, or a TV. When the first-floor apartment of the house next door was robbed, I assumed the burglars peered through our windows first, saw that there was nothing worth breaking in for and moved on.

The kitchen had no heating vents, and the space heater we dragged in to sit beside the kitchen table read thirty-nine degrees. On the weekends, friends would come over and split a twenty-four pack of Budweiser and stay up until four in the morning with their coats still on, *Sticky Fingers* and *Can't Buy a Thrill* on the turntable.

Big empty rooms and time running out. I didn't know then that you have to pay to make money: All it costs is the ability to make meaning. But being a slacker is very expensive too. All my dreaming, all my belief that I could create the life I wanted—from nothing but a Ginsberg poem and an ever-waning faith in myself—had resulted in sitting in a very cold house, with no real plan for an alternative. I wondered what everyone else had figured out that I hadn't: that making money was actually easy, or that giving your life up wasn't that bad?

"To hell with the kind of work you have to do to earn a living. All it does is fill the bellies of the pigs who exploit us," shouts a drifter to a news crew in *Slacker*. "I'll get a job when I hear the *true call*.... To all the workers out there: every single commodity you produce is a piece of your own death." The movie suggests that he may be slightly crazed but not entirely wrong.

When I turned 28, I got a new job: working in an after-school program in a very wealthy Boston suburb. I made $19 per hour for twenty-four hours a week of reading to kids, making art with them and giving them baby carrots and hummus for snacks. Three hundred and forty-four dollars a week: an absolute windfall. Since I had mornings free and our house was so cold even in early winter, I went to a café in the morning to sit in the sunny window and drink espresso.

In the LA art scene in the 60s, everybody was busy forging an important American art movement in their own image. I was just about as far from LA as you could get in the continental United States, where the winter lasted for most of the year. I was too hunched in my scarf and hat to forge American art out of my own ideals. But in the sun of the window, I felt like a plant in a greenhouse, like I might keep growing under some benevolent golden sun.

I read literature by and about important men so that maybe I could figure out how to be important too. I am one of those cursed fools who is always trying to "make meaning." Probably because I am unable to make money. I felt on some level that I would be manufacturing my own death if I gave in to the conveyor belt of capital accrual. But everyone needs *some* type of currency to live on. What could mine be? Maybe I could live like a cowboy, an economic outlaw, untethered to the pursuit of capital, stitching together enough money to get by some other way. A slacker. I hoped that if I read enough, I might be able to turn my thoughts into something that would generate some sort of value, whether it was money or meaning.

In our house, there was an unheated extra bedroom off the kitchen where we put a futon for guests. I used the room as my screenprinting studio, printing before work when it wasn't too cold to be in there. I hung a line across the room and pinned drying prints with clips: a little factory of my own.

"I am fighting a war of perseverance," Nam Jun Paik said as he worked in unheated apartments, making art no one understood. He would look like a slacker to the outsider, but in reality he was always working to create something completely new.

Austin "is to Slackerdom what the Vatican is to Christendom," declared a review of the movie. I live there now, the site of Linklater's love letter to walking around and thinking about life. I try to do that as much as I can, but mostly I have to work. The world has been transformed since I first watched *Slacker*. Sometimes I think I have been too. For money, I type sentences about payments products. It pays me enough to live and maybe one day escape. At my job, I feel as if my infinite spirit has been stuffed into a suitcase and thrown into a trunk. Corporate culture: no critical thought, just profit maximalization. The twenty-somethings I work with seem to have a jarring lack of shame about giving their lives over to a corporation, as if they know they've lost everything else, like affordable housing or a viable future on the planet, and money is the available consolation prize. No judgement, of course. To me, working for a fintech feels basically illegal, like insider trading against myself. But I've been broke for so long, and my nerves are frayed. I want the comfort of a savings account, enough money for a little warmth when it gets cold.

I was half a decade older than my young coworkers the first time I could afford a plane ticket and my rent at the same time: I felt like a millionaire. So in my thirties, tech writing emerged as a sensible option even though it left me groggy and unrecognizable to myself every day. Nailed down to a board of sorts, a balance sheet of money in and money out, and the curious feeling that the size of the number incites. Sometimes the feeling is bad, when you have to take an ambulance and worry it will cost $15,000, and sometimes it is less than bad, if you can put a couple hundred in savings and watch one number turn into a slightly larger number. But the feeling of the balance sheet is never, ever good or one of safety, satisfaction, calm or confidence. A number of many thousands, which at age 23 or 27 would have been a number big and inconceivable enough to seem like it would allow a year off from working, is still not enough. It will never be enough. A job in tech was a life raft thrown out to me that I was lucky to have: All it cost was everything I'd ever believed in. It was a pointless game I had no interest in playing, let alone winning, and I looked around the office in slight horror at everyone who seemed fine with it. Maybe they were looking at me the same way.

My boss wants to talk about my future: to strategize for a higher-paying job, a flashier title. I do not want these things. I do not want more money. I want a world where I do not have to make more money because the cost of living outpaces my raise every year. I want to lead an existence that is not similar to being trapped on an elevator that either goes ever-upward or plummets in flames to the bottom.

In a meeting it becomes clear that AI will continue to produce more of what is written in the company, which is to say, my job may disappear. This makes me anxious, but then I'm annoyed that I'm anxious: I don't even care about this job! Why would I care if a computer writes blog posts about corporate credit cards?! All my job gives me is the ability to live.

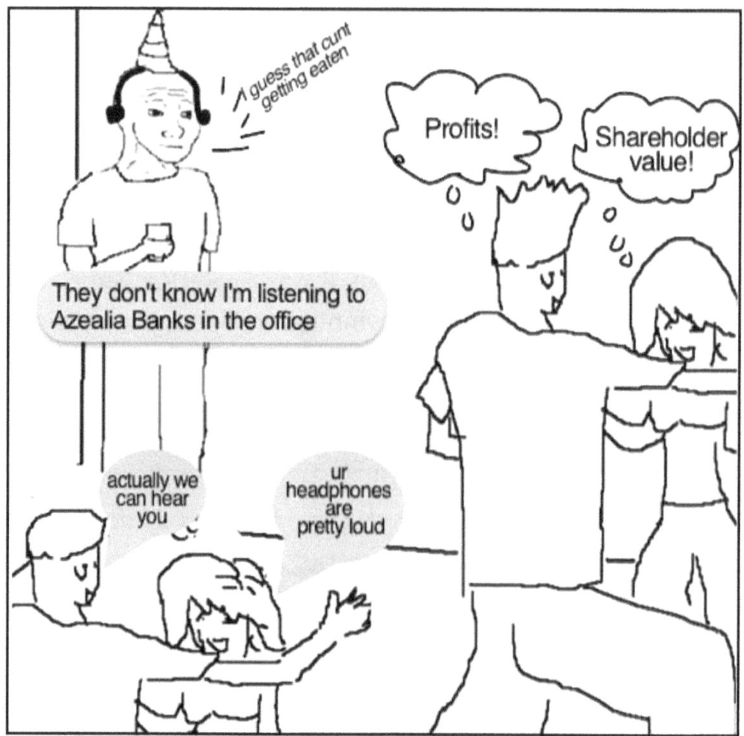

I came to Austin from a long list of cold places to leave behind the rules of life. A melancholy I'd held onto for as long as I could remember, a wistful acceptance that life would never be what it should because everything was dead for a third of the year, melted away when I came here. The palms and cacti were whimsical and insistent on living; lizards darted around the porch. The politics have degraded in the time I've lived here, but moving to Texas and complaining about the political climate is like walking into a house in flames and complaining about the heat. I was tired of the first twinges of cold descending by labor day after a too-short summer, the heat kicking on, cueing a long hibernation by Halloween and spending the next half year considering my own mortality. I wanted to wear shorts in February and believe I would never die. Mostly, it has worked. But some rules, of course, are universal.

In Austin it usually gets cold for one week a year. The bamboo lining the fence in the back of the house might become coated with ice, cracking under the weight of its new burden. Then it slowly turns a bleached wheat color and turns to a brittle mass of rattling bones. By the time I get around to spending the many hours required to chop the dead plants down and bag them up to place on the curb, it's already hot out, and by then fresh green chutes are climbing out of the ground to replace the old skeleton. In the backyard, there is also a stray palm growing next to the hose spigot—the kind of palm that looks like a fan and produces the fronds for a Palm Sunday mass. The perfect accessory to fold into a tight braid or whip your siblings with across the pew. The plant is comforting in both its familiarity and exoticism, and it regrows every year.

I go out to lunch with my coworkers, the heat of a spring afternoon already weighing heavily on us. A tall man in tailored jeans talking loudly to his earbuds strides quickly past us on the downtown Austin street. "Everyone is so business," says the intern, six months out of college. "Except for us, of course," I say as we make our way back to the office.

Austin is like most cities in 2024: it was better before you got here; it was better when we were nineteen. The buildings weren't as tall and the beer was cheaper. People like to blame newcomers,

Californians, Democrats, for ruining the city: making it more expensive, turning the downtown I bike through to get to work into a hard blue sea of gleaming glass.

At Deep Eddy, a turquoise-blue public pool off the bike trail through town, there are lots of pretty little couples on beach towels, their stick-and-poked legs wrapped around each other. The fresh bloom of new lust under the crepe myrtle trees reminds me that the world is still alive.

Rents nearly doubled in many major cities in the decade since the great recession. Is that why there are no bands anymore, and is that why I have to work in fintech? And I make more money that I ever thought I would yet still live in apartments that are slanted, poorly insulated, and still have washers and dryers older than I am. Since the recession and again in the pandemic, private equity swept like wildfire through cities, scorching everything affordable in its path. Was private equity the reason the hole-in-the-wall pizza parlor in my neighborhood, with punk posters lining the bathroom walls and a Led Zeppelin pinball machine, needs a three-million-dollar loan to stay open?

And like all cities in 2024, there is the unforgivable, omnipresent reality of homelessness. It is so prevalent and persistent and worsening I start to wonder if this crisis is engineered: the better for our overlords to indenture us with. Our neighbors lying on benches are an ever-present reminder that if we let up for one day, the bench will be ours. America seems to be bifurcated between those who have personal trainers for their dogs and those who are a surprise fifty-dollar expense away from losing stable housing for life. The message is clear: If you are not in a tall building moving a mouse to stay green on Microsoft Teams, if you let up for one second, you will be brought down to the street. As I type this now in the public library, a security guard circles to make sure that none of the men with their large suitcases beside them fall asleep at the tables or in the armchairs.

The span of my life comprises the evolution of the American populace from citizens to taxpayers. I worry that America has amounted to nothing but a new modern meanness: a hyper-competent surveillance state that would only let cops and other aspiring slaveowners alone, and the rest of us would always be suspect. Downtown at work, I have the sense that all the million ways our society has been chipped away at since the time I was born have amounted to this: people sleeping in the shadows of brand-new empty steel buildings.

And the things I used to be drawn to—around the time *Slacker* began to make sense to me as a way of life, like environmental writing, discussions of intergenerational relations, volumes of collected missives between mid-century white males—don't tempt me as much anymore. I've been thinking about environmental destruction for almost two decades—I majored in it. I've been thinking about how screwed people my age and younger are for almost as long. I'm tired of those blowhard guys who thought they knew everything. I now find the anecdote of Jack Kerouac digging a hole in the earth and fucking it while on speed less charming than I once did.

After work sometimes, I'll read about billionaires, and why and how much I should hate them, instead of listening to Dire Straits or having sex: living as an automaton cataloging dour facts about the world rather than an animal living in it. Finishing a week at work feels like a pyrrhic victory: it's Friday, and another week of my life is over and I spent it looking at my work laptop. I need something juicy, delicious, but I can't reach it or even see it from my desk. So I stay up late and have a mezcal negroni on the porch to get away with something. The people who eat carefully portioned salmon for dinner, go to bed early and hit the gym before work have always seemed to me like the perfect agents of empire: deploying their well-rested, calorie-deficient bodies each morning to increase shareholder wealth. Everyone walks around like the CEO hasn't only gained control of their head but also their heart. But this is America: Isn't misery normal? Isn't every American miserable, and the luckiest of us have a little money saved?

The best days feel overfull in their richness: work, then a walk with a detour, maybe a book or a phone call, making dinner close to ten. We spend days too busy to stare into each others' eyes unencumbered; capital has other plans. And I still need time to think and feel the summer night on my skin, slowly unwinding work's vise on my psyche. The end of the night delivers a twenty-two minute comedy, a square of chocolate, climbing into bed with our arms wrapped tightly around each other as if, if we squeezed hard enough, we would have nothing but time, to be able to revel in staying in bed late with no morning meeting. And if we didn't? We might have time to throw a brick at the state capitol and demand that—what? That they admit they are cowards, small and craven, incapable of doing anything but ruin lives? But we go to bed with tomorrow in mind, one day closer to another paycheck to spend on bills and have some left over, a luxurious form of servitude. I wait for war and for economic criminals to die and try not to think about the new ones being born.

"What it will profit me to become a good economist, I don't see," wrote James Agee while writing for Fortune Magazine. Slacker! What if the people we're calling slackers are actually very busy and very ambitious, but just not in a manner that would garner venture capitalist funding? "No one ever said slackers weren't productive," said Linklater. "It's just that their products often fall outside the market economy."

I feel the urge to remove my own head and let it sit in baking soda for a while, to wipe away the years—decades!—of grime: the hopelessness, fatigue and despair of living in the world and knowing too well how it works. But I will not scrub away the flutter of excitement at being alive. And so sometimes after work I'll put on an album I discovered during that long season of being underage and full of a different kind of malaise: breathlessly waiting for my life to start. So I will try to live my life and go for a walk around the neighborhood. Notice a redbud tree in fuller bloom than last week. Pass an adult man rolling cautiously by on a skateboard, wobbling a little as he learns: Noticing him strikes me as found poetry. We are all trying to move through the world in more novel ways.

The point of life is to find ways to feel like the opposite of being dead. Kelly says that the winners might be the people who have made peace with their impulses. I think she's right. But how can we do either when all our time is auctioned to the highest bidder? How can I transgress the boundary of the mundane to make this world worth living in? All I wanted was the sublime. Trickle-down terror is what I found. Everything feels hopeless but it can't be. Writing little things about longing seems so small but that's what we get if we're lucky: food, shelter, sleep and longing for something we can't name. Does age make us fall out of love with life, or is it the constant work that does it?

On a rainy November day I look out at the sparse trees with their dangling green and yellow leaves streaking the brown trunks and imagine it as an oil painting in front of me, and it seems like an answer to something: *How could I forget that observing the beauty of the world is the whole point!* Noticing won't solve every problem, but it will solve the problem of not being awed and romanced by that. I am constantly forgetting and remembering this. This constant process, of despairing and remembering not to and despairing again, mines all the energy of my brain, like stepping on a car's accelerator pedal when it's in park and running out the gas tank. I am wasting my time in a realm of activity that has nothing to do with who I am or what I am striving for. I have failed Linklater and betrayed myself by trying to make enough money to save and occasionally buy new shoes! I am chained to my laptop and had to learn what *buy now, pay later* is. If I was talented enough or smart enough or had enough chutzpah, I would be making brushstrokes on a canvas for a living or getting paid for my endlessly funny and illuminating observations on life and our crazy world. I would have absolutely no concept of new and innovative ways to saddle young people with consumer debt. Or am I doing the best I can with the deeply evil anti-human system that I was born into, right in the middle of Reagan's alarmingly successful war on the American people, and the people's insistence that it continue? Can anyone in America slack, take a moment, notice where they are, double back and pause before they start again? Am I living rightly, or wrongly? Richard? Are you there?

On a warm night, I can remember what it feels like to be ignited by the promise of something more, a life I would create myself. "I must create a system, or be a slave to another man's," said William Blake. A slacker? Most definitely. I search for a reprieve from the endless deluge of bills and worse news every day, the discourse on my wretched phone. I sit on the porch and try to slack, even for a few minutes: a brief, clock-free respite from a day full of hours that I have to wring money from in order to stay alive. Lester Bangs surmised that Lou Reed (slackers, both) lost his edge and would start making music about how it never rained in Southern California. What if I wrote about how it only storms in Central Texas at night? Lester also said that "all art is an act of love toward the whole human race," and when I'm in the right mood I tend to agree.

I try to write sentences of my own in an attempt at purification, to be emptied out by them: *Fuck in the afternoon, go out to a movie. Try to care about work, make time for art. Worry about Mom, worry about Elissa and the smoke in New York. Drink wine in the park, count down the days till payday. Rack up credit card bill, allot next paycheck. Tally savings, remember to watch the plants grow. Know what phase the moon is in and not what is on Twitter. Today at work I felt so dead I didn't remember what it felt like to wish I was free.*

At the end of *Slacker*, an older man walks in the early morning light speaking into a recorder, a notable diversion from the questioning twenty-somethings we've met throughout the film. "The tragedy of life is that man is never free, yet strives for what can never be," he says. He is speaking from a place of experience, of knowledge. "My life, my loves, where are they now? The necessary beauty in life is giving yourself to it completely."

This summer night, the thick air rattles like a snake. The neighbor's sprinkler casts a million little diamonds into the sky and the mosquitoes are relentless. The light of the sinking sun pours through the opening of a low cloud, the fuchsia blooms under it gathering strength until there's only a lavender pocket of fading light. I try to remember what it feels like to be alive on a hot summer evening, to feel a little free. An autonomous vehicle rounds the corner, a brainless machine circling me and my night. I watch it disappear, and I water the basil plant. The cicadas' song grows louder until it swallows the street.

You thought I wasn't going to provide a soundtrack?

Listen to the *Some Girls* playlist on Spotify:

Works quoted and referenced

This book is indebted to many works of literature, criticism, film and music including:

Some Girls

Chris Kraus quotes are from *I Love Dick* (Semiotext(e), 1998).

The quotes from Hannah Wilke are also from Kraus' research.

John Berger, *Ways of Seeing* (Penguin, 1972).

Tiqqun, *Preliminary Materials for a Theory of the Young Girl* (Semiotext(e), 2012).

Confessions of a Slutty Virgin

Oliver Stone quotes are from "Oliver Stone, a Hill alum, tells graduating seniors to go out into the world with 'wit and grit'", published in the *Pottstown Mercury*, May 25, 2013.

Agee in the Backyard

All italicized quotes are from *Let Us Now Praise Famous Men* (Houghton Mifflin, 1939)

Additional quotes from correspondence between Agee and others are from *Agee: His Life Remembered*, by Spears, Cassidy and Coles (Holt, Rinehart and Winston, 1985).

Chicago Tribune review is Bruce Allen on Genevieve Moreau's *The Restless Journey of James Agee*, published 2/27/1977.

The quote about friends never returning books is from *The Folded Clock* by Heidi Julavits (Doubleday, 2015).

Under the Paving Stones, The Beach!

Guy Debord quotes are from *The Society of the Spectacle* (Zone Books, 1995).

Other Situationist information and quotes are from *Lipstick Traces: A Secret History of the 20th Century* by Griel Marcus (Harvard University Press, 1989).

The Lawrence Weschler book referenced is *Everything that Rises: A Book of Convergences* (McSweeney's, 2007).

Gary Snyder quote is from "Smokey the Bear Sutra."

Jay Cantor quote is from *The Death of Che Guevara* (Penguin, 2005).

The Cancer horoscope is from Rob Brezsny of "Free Will Astrology."

The Allen Ginsberg quote is from "My Alba" which appears in *Reality Sandwiches* (City Lights Books, 1963).

The Henry David Thoreau quote is attributed to *Familiar Letters of Henry David Thoreau.*

Your Freedom Country

Pauline Kael quote on *Platoon* is from her *New Yorker* review which first appeared on January 12, 1987.

Local Legends

"The Why Worry Generation" by Judith Warner was published in the New York Times on May 28, 2010.

Loose Woman

The italicized passages are from Sandra Cisneros' *Loose Woman* (Vintage Contemporaries, 1995).

The Debord quote is from *Lipstick Traces*.

Slacker

The Richard Linklater quotes are from *The Austin Chronicle*, "The Art of the Interview: Self-Revelation or Self Torture? Richard Linklater Interviewed by ..." originally published September 22, 1991.

Other quotes on the movie are from "Slacking Toward Bethlehem" by Andrew Kopkind. *Grand Street*, volume 44 (1993).

The Nam Jun Paik quote is from *Moon is the Oldest TV*, 2023.

James Agee quote is from *Agee: His Life Remembered*.

The William Blake quote is attributed to *Jerusalem (1815) 'Chapter 1' (plate 10, l. 20) but I encountered it as the epigraph of Michael Azerrad's Our Band Could Be Your Life (Back Bay Books, 2001).*

Lester Bangs on Lou Reed losing his edge is from "Let Us Now Praise Famous Death Dwarves." The other quote is from "Untitled Notes on Lou Reed." Both appear in in *Psychotic Reactions and Carburetor Dung* (Vintage Books, 1998).

THANK YOU

To Mom for always believing in me and letting me win at bananagrams.

To Els for cheering me on for thirty-seven years and beyond, and everything else.

To Kelly for reading every word in here over and over for years, for listening and making it better, and for letting me quote our gchats and emails.

To Ian, for being *the* most definite article and celebrating everything with me.

To Jason Prokowiew, Kristin Amico and D.A. Navoti who have seen many of these pieces from start to finish, helped make them better, and encouraged me to keep at it.

To Breen Nolan Schoen and Heather Campbell for always providing encouragement and insight.

To Meredith Rivlin, Molly McClurg, Jack Milligan and Andrew Zarro, who have offered support to this project in a myriad of ways. And to each of my friends who have supported this book by caring about it.

To Barrett Warner for seeing something in this collection and believing in it.

To Grub Street, the Vermont Studio Center, the Mineral School, and the Southampton Writers Conference, where many of these pieces were conceived, workshopped, and written again.

To those whose work inspired the spirit and endeavor of these pieces, including Greil Marcus, Lester Bangs and Carles.

To the Bailey Howe Library, Fletcher Free Library, Multnomah County Library, Kalamazoo Public Library, Boston Public Library, and Austin Public Library, where a lifetime of reading for this book, and writing it, took place.

And to those who in all times have sought truth and who have told it in their art or their living.

About the Author

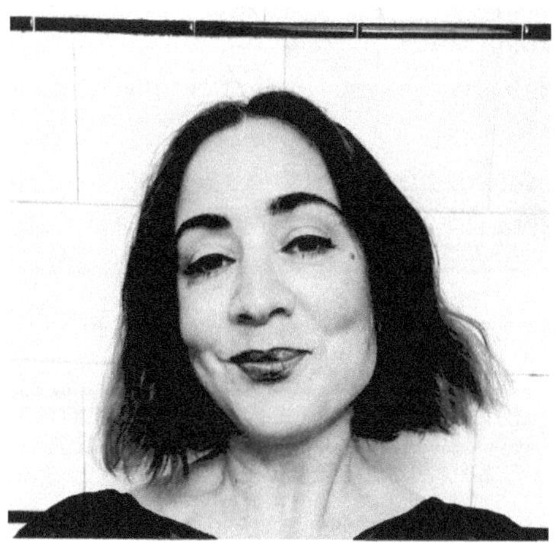

Emily May's work has been published in *Buzzfeed*, *Cagibi Lit*, *Entropy*, *espnW*, *the Hairpin*, and other venues. She sings Warren Zevon at karaoke. Visit Emily at emilyjmay.com.

About the Artist

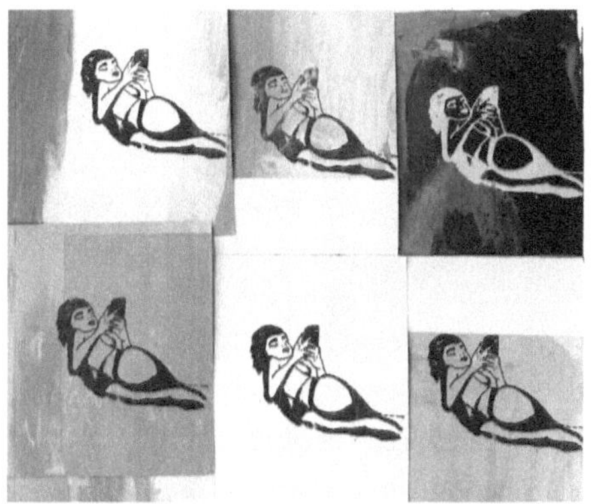

Decadent West was created in 2012 after Emily May learned to screenprint at the Kalamazoo Institute of Art. It has evolved into an ever-expanding project made from of paper goods, textiles and text. Emily is a life-long print media and fabric collector with a strong conservationist ethic: most of what she makes is sourced from re-purposed materials. Emily prints, draws, paints, collages, embroiders, sews and dreams up new ideas in her home studio in Austin.